The Dream Life Project

Laying the Foundations of Your Dream Life

CECILIA HUANG

Copyright © 2024 Cecilia Huang

thedreamlifeproject.co

ISBN:
Paperback: 978-1-923216-10-5
Ebook: 978-1-923216-11-2

All rights reserved. No parts of the publication may be reproduced, distributed, or transmitted by any person or entity, including internet search engines and retailers, in any form or by any means, electronic or mechanical, including photocopying, recording, scanning or by any information storage and retrieval system without the prior written permission from the publisher.

The views and opinions expressed in this book are those of the author, based on her personal experiences in life and business, and the book is intended to provide inspiration and valuable general guidance, however, readers must consider their own circumstances. The author makes no representation as to the suitability or validity of the content of this book to the personal circumstances of the individuals who will read the book and will not be liable for any errors, omissions, loss, damage or claims arising from the contents of this book.

Where inspirational quotations have been used, the author has used all reasonable endeavours to ensure that the materials are not in breach of copyright and intellectual property laws.

Cover design: Busybird Publishing

Layout and typesetting: Busybird Publishing

Busybird Publishing
2/118 Para Road
Montmorency, Victoria
Australia 3094
www.busybird.com.au

Dreams don't work, unless you do

John C. Maxwell

Contents

Introduction	1

Dream

Realising Your Own Dream	7
Discovering Your Purpose in Life	14
Finding Your Inner Voice	19
Staying True to Your Purpose	25
Daring To Dream Big	29

Define

Defining Your Own Success	39
Stopping Self-Sabotage in Its Tracks	46
Letting Go of Perfectionism and Embracing "Good Enough"	53
Pushing Beyond Your Comfort Zone	60
Unleashing the Fire From Within	66

Design

Why Goal-Setting Is the Secret to Success	76
Taking Ownership of Your Life	82
Planning Your Time Mindfully	89
Unstuck Yourself	96

Declutter

Decluttering Your Physical and Mental Space	105
Say Goodbye to Procrastination	111

Good Habits Will Propel Your Dream Life	117
Building and Maintaining Good Habits	125
Unearthing Your Passions in Life	131
Loving What You Do	136

Devise

Unlocking the Fullness of Life with Gratitude	147
Living in the Moment	153
Let Yourself Flow	159
Meditating for 10 Minutes Every Day	167
Working Out for 30 Minutes in the Morning	174

Develop

Regaining Self-Love	185
Eating For Your Health	192
Preventing Burnout	198
Uplifting Others to Create Positive Changes	204
Creating the Best Year of Your Life	210
One Last Thing	219
About the Author	220

Dedication

This book is dedicated to you, the reader, and my family whose support and gratitude gave me the courage to write it. Fill it with your thoughts so that it reminds you of who you really are and where you're going in life.

Introduction

After changing jobs over 20 times in 17 years of my professional career, I realised wellness should always be a top priority, as it aligns with my values and makes me excited about the life I'm living. I know exactly what it feels like to be on the daily grind, working a 9 to 5 job and feeling mentally exhausted. I've been through a journey of struggling with moving through the motions, self-sabotaging, hiding my own value, following the 'ideal' social media lifestyle, and eventually, hitting rock bottom.

If it wasn't for that Sunday night five years ago when I woke at 3:00 a.m. worrying about the imminent work tasks I had the next day, I wouldn't have dreamed about building good habits to stay positive throughout the day and week. I wouldn't have wanted to inspire millions of working women and men like you to make positive change from the inside out, to dig deep, stay on purpose, back yourself and be true to your ideas.

To live a dream life is all about 'how' to unleash your 'why'. If you have been, or are going through, such a journey, it's time to discover your true purpose in life, find out what your dream life looks like, and build good habits to make it a reality.

Imagine not just celebrating TGIF at the end of the week, but all the days in between. Imagine waking up every morning and knowing that you are truly living with intention. In this book, I share ideas and inspiration for living your best life every day. Sharing deeply personal stories, tips, and techniques to discover the 'why' in your life and build good habits to achieve it, I compel you to take your past experiences - the 'failures', the 'regrets', the 'weird times' - to thank yourself and move into your dream life.

The 30 chapters that follow are divided into six sections: dream, define, declutter, design, devise and develop. These chapters are designed to unleash your potential, explore the power of dreaming big, break free from limitations, and pursue meaningful aspirations. Ignite your imagination, set audacious goals, and embrace a life of limitless possibilities.

Keep this book by your side, and whenever you feel like you are falling off track, or feel overwhelmed, fearful, worried and anxious about life and the future, turn to these pages.

I have your back.

Learn from yesterday, cherish today, and build good habits for tomorrow. It's time to start your dream life project. Let's go.

No matter where you are from, your dreams are valid.

Lupita Nyong'o

The Dream Life Project

Dream

Dreams have long fascinated humanity, captivating our imagination as we explore realms beyond the limitations of reality. Dreams are not merely ephemeral flights of fancy. They possess the remarkable ability to guide us towards discovering our purpose in life. Dreams can offer profound insights and awaken our true aspirations, they are not merely fleeting illusions of the night, but windows into our innermost selves. By exploring our dreams, deciphering their messages, and embracing their transformative power, we can uncover our passions, overcome limitations, and ignite our purpose in life. Embrace the wisdom of your dreams, act on them as they lay the roadmap to a fulfilling, meaningful and purpose-driven life.

Realising Your Own Dream

Are you truly living a life of purpose?

Purpose clarifies why we do what we do, helps us set goals and motivates us to achieve them. Determining what our purpose is in life can be one of the hardest things that we have to do. Every year, especially in December, I ask myself three questions:

1. What is my purpose?

2. How do I find out the 'why' in my life?

3. Why do I do what I do?

I found that my purpose has changed throughout my life, and I bet you found the same. If you haven't spent a lot of time thinking about your own purpose, you might have some preconceived ideas about the purpose of life. These baked-in ideas about life often come from our family and the communities we grow up in. The purpose could be to get married and have kids. Or maybe it's earning a certain amount of money or achieving a certain position in society.

But these types of achievements often don't bring the fulfilment that comes with finding your personal sense of purpose. A personal sense of purpose is less of a specific end goal and more of an ongoing impact on the world, large or small.

Purpose is your why.

This personal sense of purpose guides and sustains you, day to day and year to year. Even when you have setbacks and the world turns upside down, purpose gives you stability and a sense of direction. That's why finding purpose is essential for living a happy, healthy life.

Your purpose in life is as unique to you as your fingerprint. It is why you get out of bed in the morning, even when the day is dreary, you're tired, and you know the tasks and challenges ahead are going to be hard or boring.

Your purpose resides in the overlap between what you love and what you are good at. Purpose is the long game, not the short-term goal; you need a sense of purpose to sustain you over time. Even when life feels like a series of compromises, you can still discover and connect to your purpose by exploring what brings you joy and dedicating more time to it.

Living a meaningful life contributes to better physical health and mental fitness. It also reduces the risk of chronic disease. Multiple studies have even found that it can help you live longer.

When you want to pursue something, you need to know what it is about. you need to know what you are dreaming about, and what your dream life is. So, what's your dream? What gives you that kick in the morning? What are the things you want to dedicate yourself to?

Many people don't even dare to dream; they are fearful of dreaming. They think that dreaming is childish; that as grown-up people, they should not dream. Your dream is your goal in life. Who do you want to become in 10 years? How do you want to be remembered by your friends and family? Use these six questions to help you set up your goals and visualise your dream life. They can help speed up making your dream a reality.

1. What do you want to achieve in 10 years?

What's most important for you to experience, explore or embrace this time around? Until you answer this question, your life goals will be off-purpose. If your inner passion doesn't align with your intentions, you won't have the power to attract the people and situations necessary to make it a reality.

Get clued to your true joy. What activities did you enjoy as a child? What are your hobbies now? When your goals are aligned with your soul, synchronicity kicks in to guide you to your target. Write your answer down, it will be part of your dream life vision board.

2. Is this your dream or someone else's?

Are your goals your own, or what others think you should strive for? Do you want to look back in your old age and wish you had followed your passion? Will you regret having 'played it safe'?

Chasing your own dreams is never selfish. You deserve a journey full of passion, joy and happiness, and to live a purposeful and intentional life. Define your own dream, not someone else's.

3. Are you settling for less?

Are you resigned to accepting less than your full share of love, health and success in this lifetime? Have you compromised and sacrificed your dream?

If you found yourself settling for less, why? Is it due to a lack of money, being short of time, or not receiving enough support? You can always find time out of the day, squeeze one dollar out of your daily expenses, and join a new circle of supportive people.

Please remember, anything short of pursuing your true passions will never make you happy.

4. What will reaching your dream feel like?

Personal passion fuels a vision. Dive into the thrill and exhilaration of the feeling of living your dream. Recall a moment when you achieved a goal. The excitement, and the thrill is so great that you can never forget them. Make these moments happen over and over again. Where your creative attention flows, so does your life.

5. What steps can you take today toward your dream?

Don't defer your dream. Set up supports and systems around you to instantly translate your intentions into action. Jump on every opportunity that is in line with your purpose and vision.

Surround yourself with great people, those who can coach you through the journey, motivate you, inspire you, and propel you to move forward. Join The Dream Life Project community for your daily dose of inspiration.

Are there smaller projects you can do that can lead to your larger dream? If your dream is to run a marathon, train for a local fun-run first. Find a way to measure your progress. Take time, think deeply, and track those little wins by writing in a journal.

6. Do you tell yourself, 'I can't have my dream'?

Most people don't believe they can pursue their dreams. Either their belief system has them believing they can't make a living doing what they love, or they feel they don't deserve their dream. To avoid the pain of feeling like they can't have their dream, people often keep their dream deeply buried, and eventually, they can't remember they ever had a dream.

Yes, you can have a dream. Tell yourself to dream big. Only when you can dream it, can you do it. Your dream life is closer than you think.

Everyone has a dream! And everyone is destined to fulfil that purpose. Why wait?

Knowing yourself is the beginning of all wisdom.

Aristotle

Discovering Your Purpose in Life

To have a purpose is to feel connected with your dream life. It gives you a reason to get out of bed each morning. If you are asking yourself, "what is my purpose?" I'd love to share my eight tips to get started on finding purpose in life.

1. Develop a growth mindset

Having a growth mindset is linked to having a sense of purpose. When things go wrong, a growth mindset helps you preserve self-esteem and giving you the resilience to push forward. It helps maintain optimism about the future, and that underlying belief that you can do it. Constantly growing and becoming a better version of yourself helps you identify your purpose and commit to pursuing it.

A growth mindset also allows you to:

- Embrace challenges as opportunities.
- Persevere in spite of failure.
- Accept feedback and constructive criticism.

2. Create a personal vision statement

A personal vision statement can help you manage stress and find balance in your life. It also serves as a roadmap that will guide you toward your purpose by identifying your core values and establishing what's important to you.

It allows you to make decisions that are aligned with your values and helps you stay motivated as you work toward your personal goals.

3. Feel grateful for what life offers

Being grateful can reduce toxic emotions, from resentment and envy to regret and frustration. Gratitude effectively increases happiness and reduces depression. Additionally, grateful people experience fewer aches and pains, and feel healthier and get better sleep. There are also surprising connections between how well our food is digested relative to our attitude. Research shows that taking a moment to be thankful causes physiological changes in your body that initiate the part of your nervous system that helps you rest and digest, the parasympathetic nervous system. Gratitude helps to bring down your blood pressure, heart rate and breathing.

To get started with feeling more relaxed, try writing three to five things you feel grateful for first thing in the morning or at the end of your day.

4. Explore your passions

Your passions and interests are a good indicator of the area in which your life purpose might lie, although they can be hard to identify. They're so ingrained in our ways of thinking that we can become blind to them.

If you're not sure what your passions are, ask the people who know you best. Likely, you're already pursuing them in some way without even realising it.

Another way to find your passion is to think about what you're good at. You might prefer to keep your passion as a hobby, or you might decide to turn it into a side hustle or primary source of income.

5. Spend time with people who inspire you

You are the average of the five people you spend the most time with. If you spend time with people who are positive and purpose-driven, they are likely to inspire you to have the same mindset. You may even discover your purpose through them.

Look beyond your colleagues and family members and ask yourself who you choose to spend your time with. Evaluate those relationships and make sure you are surrounding yourself with aspirational, positive people who uplift you.

6. Listen to podcasts

One of the best ways to expand your mental horizon is through listening to podcasts. It helps you improve your empathy and critical and creative thinking. I love to tune into a new podcast episode after work to listen to other people's stories and get inspiration. Podcasts are nothing new, but it wasn't until recently that I built a daily habit of listening to them. It was a time when I was looking for joy in any and every way I could find it.

7. Practice self-acceptance

Accepting your limitations can help you be kinder to yourself when things go wrong. We all make mistakes, but instead of beating yourself up for your failures, try to see each setback as an opportunity to grow.

Self-compassion can help you become more self-aware and self-accepting. When you accept all of yourself, you're more likely to give the best of yourself in every situation. This might be at work, with your family, or while doing the things you love.

This can lead to a greater sense of connection to others and everything you do, giving more meaning to your life.

8. Take time for self-care

Self-care comes in many forms, and your version of self-care is unique to you. Perhaps you like walking in the forest, practising breathwork, or journaling out your difficult emotions.

But why is self-care important? Because when our brains are relaxed, they are at their most creative. You cannot achieve or serve others when you are battling against yourself.

Creative thinking comes naturally when our minds are in a state of relaxation, and it can lead you closer to finding your purpose.

The two most important days of your life are the day you were born and the day you find out why.

Mark Twain

Finding Your Inner Voice

Our inner voice is our innate intelligence. When we listen to it, we turn inward to hear what our body and soul have to say before looking to the world outside for direction.

Whether your inner voice is loud and clear or more of a whisper, listening to it can be a great source of guidance. You can think of your inner voice as akin to your highest self. It's that wise part of you that can float high above the details of the moment, your own emotions, and the emotions of others to get an eagle-eye view of your life.

Whether your inner voice is responding to a present situation, reflecting on an experience, or helping to guide you in the future. It is the voice of truth, your unique voice of truth that comes from within.

Practice listening to your inner voice

Allowing your inner voice to guide you can help you become the best version of yourself. It will help you fully discern your wisdom, guidance, and direction; there's nothing more powerful than trusting yourself and confidently following your truth.

In my own life, I have found my inner voice to be the most crucial guide. It's instilled within me a deep trust that I can count on myself and my experience to guide me through life. This feeling is priceless.

If listening to your inner voice is new to you, it can feel difficult to tap into, especially if there are a lot of outward demands for your time and attention. Here are some tips to start accessing your inner voice:

1. Create space in your life

When you're rushing through your days, the mind can race too, so make sure you're giving yourself time to slow down. The best way to tap into your inner voice is to create more space between your thoughts and clear your headspace.

2. Set boundaries

Strong boundaries are essential in so many areas of our lives, particularly if you're trying to access your inner voice. Nothing will override your inner voice more than letting other people's thoughts, demands, needs, desires, and authority outweigh your own. So, learn how to say no, check in with yourself before saying yes to anything, and learn to trust yourself.

3. Get curious about fleeting moments of insight

Your inner voice is so easy to ignore. It is a subtle feeling, a quiet knowing and a gentle guidance system. It will not override the decision for you, you will still need to make decisions based on your sensible analysis and judgement.

It's easy to brush over an 'aha' moment, a wave of goosebumps or a weirdly specific dream, but the more we learn to pay attention to these instances, the better we become at discerning and understanding them.

4. Mind your physical and mental health

If you want to access your higher knowing, you need to make sure your baseline needs are taken care of too. Get whatever emotional support you need from loved ones and professionals. Additionally, maintaining more balance in your physical body through a healthy diet and moderate exercise can help you to feel more nourished. When your system feels balanced, it can be easier to discern the difference between your inner voice and an emotional reaction. If something goes wrong with a part of your nervous system, you can have trouble moving, speaking, swallowing, breathing, or learning. You may also have problems with your memory, senses, or mood.

5. Spend some time tech-free

Allow yourself to try be alone in silence with fewer distractions. Turn off phones, computers, and other screens for a minimum of one hour per day. Don't try to force your inner voice to speak to you, rather create the conditions required for deep inner listening; it will come to you.

6. Try journaling in the morning

Journaling three handwritten pages each morning will become a stream of consciousness. Write anything that comes to mind to get going, and usually by the end of the third page, your inner voice will reveal a clear and concrete direction for the day.

My philosophy is: it's none of my business what people say about me and think of me. I am what I am and I do what I do.

Anthony Hopkins

Staying True to Your Purpose

Life is full of ups and downs. When things go wrong or don't go as planned, or when something happens to throw us off balance and doubt ourselves, it can be tough to deal with. It's not what happens to you but what you do with what happens to you that makes the difference.

Seven years ago, I left a job that I'd been in for three years for a better offer. I was fired from the new job after only two months. Without any constructive feedback or prior notice from my new employer, I woke up without a job. Obviously, this job change didn't turn out to be a better offer; quite the opposite, in fact. I couldn't control the outcome of a job change no matter how hard I worked. All I could do was leave the bad experience behind, change my perspective, and tell myself, "I'm worth it!" Did I lose out and become scared of changing jobs? Nope, one week later, I flipped the negative into the positive and started a new job-hunting journey. Since then, I've changed jobs another four times, and they all worked out well, with each offer better than the last.

I learned some lessons from this experience. I'm sharing my ways so that you will never lose out again, and always stay on purpose.

1. **Focus on your strengths**

We have a whole load of strengths and weaknesses that affect what we do and how we do it, but we tend to put more focus on our weaknesses and not our strengths.

A strength is something that you do consistently well, something you're able to do with minimum effort. You're hard-wired to do it well and you get an inherent satisfaction from doing it. It could be tackling and solving complex problems, empathising with people, having a lively imagination or being able to make the perfect omelette.

Focusing on what you do well rather than what you're not so good at makes all the difference. When you look at what you're not good at, you feel bad about yourself and your ability, but when you focus on and play to your strengths, you're guaranteed to get results and can even eliminate any negative effect your weaknesses might have.

2. Take actions towards your desired outcome

Get really clear on the outcome you want and how it would feel to get what you're looking for. Then start breaking it down: what can you do to set things up so that your desired outcome happens? What needs to be put in place? What will help to make what you want happen? To ensure the best outcome, what are the efforts and investments you are willing to put into it?

3. Set the right goals

Take time to dive into yourself as far as you can. Morning is the best time to clear your mind from thoughts of the daily grind and dedicate some time to find your purpose in the fresh breeze. Before a hectic day starts, enjoy a cuppa, put a pen on paper, write down your thoughts: define your core values (and limits), and draw a clear vision of where you are heading.

4. Achieve a work/life balance

Work/life balance is the secret recipe to professional and personal success. The balance between these two is pivotal for leading a dream life. There is no magic wand to achieve it, you just need to prioritise those things that will get you to your goals and know when and what trade-offs are to be made.

5. Find your daily affirmation

When you start feeling like you've lost your direction or motivation, or you've forgotten what your purpose is, find an affirmation that speaks to you and seek wisdom from people who have gone through a similar journey.

The more often you do this and check in on yourself, the more certain you will feel on track - on purpose - and driving towards the big dreams you want to achieve. It's important to have a daily habit that allows you to tune into your innate strength.

I truly believe each day holds the promise of a fresh start, the chance to hit the reset button and seize the opportunity to grow taller and stronger. Find inspiration, thoughts and guidance for dealing with the challenges and new experiences around work and business, relationships, family, friendship, self-esteem and your connection to the world. Affirmations encourage you to take the leap of faith and find something greater than yourself.

Find something you are passionate about and keep tremendously interested in it.

Julia Child

Daring To Dream Big

If you can dream it, you can do it. To live your life to the fullest, one key factor you need to remember is the size of your dreams. If your dreams are small, you will miss many things in life. You will miss them not because they are out of your reach, but because your limiting beliefs hinder you from reaching them.

That's why I believe it's important that we learn to dream big. Life is too precious to be spent pursuing small dreams. Dream big so that you can reach your full potential. To dream big, you need to make sure you pursue the right dreams, those which are both fulfilling and meaningful.

A dream is an idea or vision that is created in your imagination or something that you have wanted very much to do, be, or have for a long time.

A big dream is a substantial wish or an aspiration for something, which when you attain it, you believe would fulfill or satisfy an inner longing or desire.

A big dream is a bold vision of the future, a vision that both scares and excites you at the same time. It brings out your passion, imagination, creativity and willingness to take and embrace risks. A big dream is a fire in your belly that fills you up with a craving to make yourself better.

The Dreaming Process

The dreaming process revolves around answering four important questions: what, why, when, and how?

- **What do you want to achieve?**

- **Why do you want to achieve it?**

- **When do you want to achieve it?**

- **How will you achieve it?**

Knowing what your big dream is, why you want to achieve it and when is a very powerful driving force. The 'what', 'why' and 'when' are usually fairly easy to identify and define.

The 'how' can take anywhere from a few seconds to a lifetime to figure out.

Your reason 'why' will keep you going when nobody else believes in you. It is that gut instinct that will strengthen you and keep you in the race when you feel tempted to give up.

Your big dream is your personal internal compass that guides you through your life's journey.

Write Down Your Big Dream

You should write down your big dream. The very act of writing it down signifies a commitment to yourself that you are willing to do what it takes to achieve your dream. It makes the pledge real in your mind.

You should be very clear and specific regarding what your dream is, what you want to achieve, why you want to achieve it, how you will achieve it, and how you will measure the progress.

Develop a vision board for your dream. Your big dream should make you excited and afraid at the same time. Close your eyes, fast forward into the future and imagine that you have accomplished your dream. What would it feel like?

Write down a detailed description of what your end goal looks like. What kind of person will you be in 10 years?

Specify what is important to you. Have a bright and clear vision. Be a risk taker, go against the grain. You do not have to fit in to achieve your dreams.

Set Goals for Your Big Dream

The next step after you have written down your dream is to develop smaller goals that all feed into your big dream. Break down your big dream into specific goals, small tasks and milestones. For example, if you have a 20-year dream, you can break this down into 10, 5, 1 year, 6 month, quarterly and monthly goals.

Categorise your goals into a few long-term (more than a year) and a few short-term (less than a year) objectives. Identify which actions you have to take in order to achieve your goals and break down the big actions into smaller tasks.

Translate monthly and quarterly goals into a series of daily or weekly tasks. Aim to do one small task every day or at least every week that is related to achieving your big dream.

Assign a timeframe to the different goals and tasks. Identify what skills and resources you will need. Prioritise the goals so that you know which ones to focus on first.

Devise a way to measure how the goals are being accomplished. This will help in tracking your progress. Additionally, keep track of the tasks that you are doing that add up to a specific goal or milestone.

Give yourself deadlines for achieving your overall dream, and accomplishing each of your goals.

Read your dreams regularly to refresh yourself, keep you focused and evaluate your progress. Keep reminding yourself of the reasons why you are pursuing your big dream. Your reasons are the driving force that will keep you persevering.

Revise and update your goals on an annual basis and realign them based on current and evolving circumstances.

The future belongs to those who believe in the beauty of their dreams.

Eleanor Roosevelt

Scan the QR code or visit thedreamlifeproject.co website for additional resources, including downloadable journals, meditations and podcasts.

Define

In our quest for a meaningful life, we often find ourselves chasing external markers of success prescribed by society. However, true fulfilment lies in defining success on our own terms. It liberates us from the confines of societal expectations and unlocks the path to a meaningful life. By delving into our values, setting purposeful goals, and embracing the journey, we create a life that aligns with our authentic selves. Defining success can be the catalyst for a fulfilling life and embarking on the journey of discovering the profound joy and purpose that awaits us.

The Dream Life Project

Defining Your Own Success

How do you define success?

I'll probably hear completely different answers from every person. For some people, success is a matter of having a big house and a nice car. Others may point to success coming from meaningful work, a fulfilling job that feeds their passion, or strong relationships with friends and family.

There is no right answer to this question. To begin, let's start at the root of the question: what is success?

As a starting point, it's helpful to know that success is typically defined as reaching a goal or accomplishing something you've set out to achieve. It provides a source of motivation for people to change their lives and values.

There are all kinds of strategies, ways of thinking, patterns of behaviour and practical tips to be successful, improve your life and feel better about yourself, but they're all redundant if the foundation isn't there. That foundation is the real you, the you that you know deep down, your core values and your true definition of success.

My favourite definition of success is a quote from a respected coach and teacher, John Wooden:

"Success is peace of mind that is the direct result of self-satisfaction in knowing you did your best to become the best that you are capable of becoming."

The trick is that it takes time and courage to find that and to bring out who you are. Here are three key steps to help you define your own success.

1. Get to know your values

A value is something in yourself, in others or in the world that's most important to you, and could include things like beliefs, progress, family, fun, nature, achievement or freedom. Your value will only make sense to you; it defines who you are, where you come from and where you want to head to.

Personal values are a big passion of mine and I often get carried away when I talk about them. They're one of the most important things you can know about yourself and are vital in building genuine inner confidence. Your values are one thousand kilometres down inside you, right at the very core of who you are. They're the building blocks, the foundations and cornerstones of *you*.

Why is it that some people and situations leave you feeling angry, frustrated, demotivated or deflated? It's because one or more of your values is being denied, suppressed or repressed. As humans, we experience that as a negative experience because it's denying a fundamental piece of who you are.

Your values are all yours, and no matter what happens, no one can ever take them away. You can have absolute confidence in them because they're unique to you, but it takes time for you to notice and use them.

When you get to know your values, you can start to make choices and align your life around them. Once you find that alignment, it feels amazing! You start allowing yourself to be who you are.

2. Ask yourself: "what does success look like?"

Confidence builds up from what you've achieved, your accomplishments and your success. Before you start striving for success, it's important to identify exactly what it means to you. And, just as importantly, how you will measure the way success is unfolding in your life.

It's crucial to identify your own criteria when you devote your energy and effort to a project, like what I'm doing with The Dream Life Project. You will feel that success is your complete body of work in life.

- **How does success feel to you?**

- **How will you measure it daily?**

- **How would you define success in one sentence?**

So, what you are after is a new, sustainable formula for success that allows you to embrace everything you are today. You make a huge number of choices on a day-to-day basis that determines how successful you are, and it's up to you to recognise this. Tapping into your feeling of success every day will keep you motivated and inspired.

Here are some examples of success to help you get started:

- **Success means I can work from anywhere, at any time.**

- **Success is the ability to earn a living from work that I'm passionate about.**

- **Success means I'm able to give back to my community.**

- **Success is ticking off all my tasks on my to-do lists and enjoying a relaxing bubble bath.**

Now over to you. Write down your own definition of success. How would you define success in one sentence?

3. Say NO to things that can't get you to your success

Many people, especially women, struggle to say 'no' for fear of sounding rude. But it's a vital skill that helps you stay on track to achieving your success so that your energy won't be drained by negativities that happen in life.

To set goals that help you achieve your success, you first need to know yourself better. Take time to dive and withdraw into yourself as far as you can. Journaling in the morning helps you to clear your mind, set your intention and get ready to unveil a hectic day. Know your core values, define your limits, and draw a clear vision of where you are heading.

Answering the following 10 questions is the first step towards finding out why you do what you do. Don't rush this exercise, you don't need to complete it in one morning. Take as much time as you need, your essence will help you uncover your purpose.

1. **What makes you tick? What do you wake for each morning?**

2. **What truly inspires you?**

3. **How do you want to be known in 10 years?**

4. **What difference will others say you made in this world?**

5. **How do you want to feel every day?**

6. **What are your innate strengths?**

7. **What are your non-negotiables in life?**

8. What are you good at?

9. What do you want to achieve in life?

10. How do you want to add great value to the things you do?

When your values are clear to you, making decisions is easier.

– Roy E. Disney

Stopping Self-Sabotage in Its Tracks

The other day, I found myself rushing so much that I ended up forgetting my phone charger. I had back-to-back meetings while I was on the road, and I wouldn't be able to dial in if my phone battery is flat. What's worse, it turned out that I'd gotten an important call and I spent the entire time feeling anxious about my phone dying. Have you been in a similar situation to mine?

To stop sabotaging yourself, you must first recognise when it's getting in your way. Sometimes, you're acutely and painfully aware of this, like when you find yourself procrastinating to write an important email to your client and knowing that multiple tasks are due on the same day. Or, you impulsively buy a large bag of potato chips when you're trying to cut back on junk food.

What Is Self-Sabotage?

Self-sabotage refers to the beliefs and behaviours that prevent you from achieving your goals, hopes, and dreams. It is a very normal part of the human experience, something we all do from time to time, often without fully realising we're doing it.

At its core, self-sabotage involves any attitude or behaviour that doesn't match up with your values and interferes with your ability to achieve your life goals. We all do things from time to time that get in the way of our progress, but self-sabotage is a pattern of thoughts and actions that create ongoing problems, preventing us from moving forward and facing change successfully.

When you self-sabotage, you regularly engage in self-defeating behaviours like procrastination, perfectionism, negative self-talk, avoidance, or conflict. Often driven by anxiety, fear, and self-doubt, they undermine your efforts to build your dream life. Self-sabotage becomes especially problematic when the behaviour becomes a habit, done so automatically that you don't even fully realise you're doing it, or that it is leading directly to negative consequences.

11 Signs You're Self-Sabotaging

1. Avoiding people and situations that make you uncomfortable.

2. Staying within your comfort zone and avoiding change.

3. Setting goals that are too low to ensure success.

4. Creating conflict with your partners, loved ones, friends, or co-workers.

5. Trying to control others.

6. Attempting to gain others' approval.

7. Making excuses.

8. Taking actions that don't match your values and goals.

9. Comparing yourself to others.

10. Social withdrawal or isolation.

11. Risky behaviours (such as substance use, gambling, overspending, or promiscuity).

How Self-Sabotaging Behaviour Impacts Your Life

Self-sabotaging behaviour disrupts your progress toward achieving your goals and can prevent you from living a life you truly value. Some people get in the way of their own happiness and success in one particular area, while others impede themselves in several different areas. Common life realms that fall prey to self-sabotage include romantic relationships, careers, education, and relationships with family and friends.

Here are three ways that self-sabotage can impact your life:

1. Self-sabotaging your romantic relationships

Sometimes people do things that undermine their long-term romantic relationships, by engaging in behaviours that ultimately lead to a breakup. Often born out of fear of loss, romantic self-sabotage can involve blaming, picking fights, giving the silent treatment, attempting to control or monitor a partner's behaviour, constantly seeking reassurance, clinginess, having impossibly high expectations, and leaving relationships before they have a chance to develop.

2. Self-sabotaging your career

Self-sabotaging your career involves actions that prevent you from achieving your career goals. Fear of failure or anxiety about uncertainty can trap you in your comfort zone and prevent you from advancing despite having a desire to do so. This leads to unhappiness at work that negatively affects your mental health and wellbeing. It can also lead to frequent job changes.

3. Self-sabotaging your relationships with friends & family

This type of self-sabotage is often driven by a sense of competition that comes from a need to prove your worth, equality, or superiority. Negative behaviour that interferes with positive relationships with loved ones might involve passive-aggressive behaviour, clinginess, false compliments, approval-seeking, boasting, constant explaining, or frequent check-ins to see if others are angry or otherwise upset with you.

Seven Tips For Stopping Self-Sabotage:

1. Boost your self-awareness

Spend time in self-reflection to increase your self-awareness of your own self-sabotaging. Try journaling regularly to document your behaviours and thought patterns; see if you can identify where they are coming from. Pause several times throughout the day to check in with yourself. As you develop insight about yourself, you can become more intentional about where you need to make changes.

2. Identify what's holding you back

As you notice negative behaviours, thoughts, and feelings, ask yourself whether these habits are helping you or hurting you. Often, we feel pressured to do something or avoid doing something out of fear, so taking a moment to decide if something will hold you back or move you forward can prevent self-sabotage.

3. Set meaningful goals and develop an action plan

Meaningful goals help you live with purpose. To achieve these goals, develop a plan outlining specific actions. Consider your deepest values when setting your goals. What do you want more of in your life? What creates a sense of meaning and purpose? What makes you feel energised and alive? Then, decide what small steps you can take to move toward a goal.

4. Take small steps, one at a time

Positive action certainly beats self-defeating action but remember that habits are most effectively changed in small steps. Think in terms of making incremental change. Replace one thought or behaviour every day and give yourself time to make that change a habit.

5. Befriend with yourself

The inner critic is a primary factor underlying self-sabotage; therefore, replacing automatic, self-critical thoughts with more nurturing ones is a crucial step in stopping it. Develop a gentle, accepting attitude toward yourself by acknowledging your emotions and accepting past mistakes.

6. Know & embrace your strengths

Everyone has character strengths that can help them thrive, so acknowledge and embrace them. Reflect on your strengths, identifying not just things you do well but attitudes you hold dear and positive emotions you experience. When do you feel your best? Knowing your strengths and finding ways to use them at least once every day can help you beat self-sabotage.

7. Practice mindfulness

Mindfulness involves being fully present and grounded in each moment. It helps you separate the past from the present and thoughts from reality. It challenges negative self-talk habits, and, in turn, helps you choose how to respond to a problematic situation or person.

The only thing that will stop you from fulfilling your dreams is you.

Tom Bradley

Letting Go of Perfectionism and Embracing "Good Enough"

Perfectionism is the drive to be perfect. If you're a perfectionist, you may have a high personal standard you set for yourself and tell yourself that nothing is ever good enough. You may also judge your self-worth based on your ability to achieve this standard.

Being a perfectionist is often seen as a strength of character or having a good work ethic. Perfectionism usually stems from believing our self-worth is determined by our achievements. It can rob us of our self-esteem and make life feel less enjoyable because perfectionists are more likely to experience decreased productivity, impaired health, troubled interpersonal relationships, and low self-esteem. Perfectionists are also vulnerable to depression and anxiety.

If you found yourself doing a task, anything less than perfect makes you not want to complete it at all, and you feel hopeless about finding ways to help ease the stress and anxiety of trying so hard to be perfect, you could be a perfectionist.

How Perfectionism Holds Us Back

1. Perfectionism keeps us from pushing beyond our comfort zone

For perfectionists, an implicit and false notion swirls in our heads: "If I don't master it immediately, I won't like it, so I won't try it." We want to do it perfectly right away, so if we have a sense we won't be good at it, we usually just avoid it. Not pushing beyond our comfort zone means missing out on some enjoyable experiences and potentially missing out on something we could be good at.

At its worst, perfectionism distracts us from revelling in the process because we're so focused on the finish line. Not only does this keep us from experiencing new things or trying our hand at new activities, hobbies, or jobs, but perfectionism keeps us from personal growth which can potentially lead to our dream life.

2. Perfectionism stops us from experiencing failure

While avoiding failure might sound like a good thing at first, failure is a normal, important part of life. Failure helps us build adaptability and resilience, so avoiding failure stops us from building our abilities.

Perfectionists are very good at conquering challenges that are still within their skill area. Perfectionists know which challenges are outside their area of expertise or skill and know how to avoid them. However, when we don't experience small failures, we don't know how to handle the bigger failures of life, or the real and inevitable adversity life throws at us.

3. Perfectionism often drives procrastination

Not trying new things and avoiding failure are why perfectionists are often procrastinators. We put off starting something new out of an internal fear of not doing it well. Perfectionists can often pull off a last-minute feat, work hard and accomplish the goal. Though this may sound like a good thing, procrastination fuels anxiety and can lead to poor health habits, such as chronic sleep deprivation and stress. Procrastination also doesn't allow us the time to go over our projects or work, keeping us from revising, catching mistakes, or making it even better.

4. Perfectionism keeps us feeling like we're not enough

Perfectionism keeps us relying on the approval of others to give us our worth: be it in feedback, praise, monetary compensation, or awards and prestige. Perfectionism stays alive when we look for other people to give us worth, relying on their opinions to give us a sense of our value. However, a real, personal sense of worthiness can never come from others, it can only come from ourselves. In this case, we are essentially putting our self-worth in the hands of others. Only when we receive positive feedback, do we set new goals, striving for perfection (yet again) because we struggle to affirm ourselves as good enough or having done enough.

5. Perfectionism fuels anxiety

Perfectionism is fuelled by setting nearly unattainable standards for ourselves, as well as looking to other people or to external metrics of success to give us our worth. With the constant pressure of striving to reach high goals and impress others, perfectionism often leads to an underlying, or even overwhelming, sense of anxiety.

This pervasive anxiety is usually fuelled by a little voice inside our heads. This "voice" may be the voice of someone in our lives that we have internalised, such as a critical parent or a never-satisfied authority figure. Regardless of where this internal critic originated from, its persistence can fuel social anxiety, performance anxiety, and/or general anxiety. It keeps telling us that we are not enough and that we need to do more and achieve more.

How To Cope With Perfectionism

Several helpful tips can help you manage or break the cycle of perfectionism. Here are a few steps to consider.

1. Be aware of your thoughts

To overcome or manage perfectionism, you need to become aware of your thoughts and behaviours. Journaling can help you identify them. Pick a time when you've grappled with perfectionism and write down any thought that comes to mind around the task that you felt you needed to do perfectly, whether it feels rational or not. As you write down your thoughts, what themes start to show? Once you identify the thoughts, themes, and behaviours, then you can start to change them.

2. Allow yourself to make mistakes

When you allow yourself to make mistakes, it teaches your brain that it's not the end of the world if you fail. A mistake is a perfect opportunity to learn, grow and do better.

Try something you've never tried before, and instead of trying to be perfect, try to focus on enjoying it or learning how to get better. This will help you learn that mistakes are necessary to get to where you want to be.

3. Alter your negative self-talk

If you're constantly thinking that you're not good enough, then it can be hard to overcome perfectionism. This negative self-talk that goes on in your mind can be detrimental to your self-esteem. By altering your self-talk, you can have a more positive effect on your self-esteem, which can lead to the dream life you are working towards.

4. Practice embracing "good enough"

Perfectionism is an unrealistic expectation. It may come from an emotional place deep inside of you. Your mind may try to convince you that your work is not good enough yet. Try to acknowledge and understand that you have perfectionistic tendencies. If you've completed a task and you know you've done a good job, practice accepting that while it may not be perfect, it is good enough.

You don't have to be great to start, but you have to start to be great.

Zig Ziglar

Pushing Beyond Your Comfort Zone

The ability to take risks by stepping outside our comfort zone is the primary way by which we grow, but we are often afraid to take that first step.

Comfort zone are about fear rather than comfort. Break the chains of fear to get outside the comfort zone. Once you do, you will learn to enjoy the process of taking risks and growing in the process.

When my manager asked me to step up to be the team leader, my first reaction was "I can't." I can't attend the team calls at midnight, I can't bear the additional supervision and administrative responsibilities, and I can't manage the expectations of other stakeholders. This translates to: I can't push beyond my comfort zone.

After two weeks of evaluating the opportunity and the challenges, I told myself "I can do it." I can ask someone to record the midnight calls so I can watch the playback during the day. I can delegate some of my tasks to an agency to save time on add-on responsibilities. I can set up regular meetings with the stakeholders to discuss work in progress and check their expectations.

It turned out I CAN!

I want to share with you my thought process of flipping "can't do" into "can do."

1. Become aware of what's outside of your comfort zone

What are the things that you believe are worth doing but are afraid of doing because of the potential for disappointment or failure?

To combat the fear, I draw a circle and write down those things that I'm uncomfortable with outside the circle. Then, I write comforts inside the circle. This process not only allows me to clearly identify my discomforts but also, my comforts. See if it does the same for you.

2. Become clear about what you are aiming to overcome

Take the list of discomforts and go deeper. Remember, the primary emotion you are trying to overcome is fear.

How does this fear apply uniquely to each situation? Be very specific.

Are you afraid of walking up to people and introducing yourself in social situations? Why? Is it because you are insecure about the sound of your voice? Are you insecure about the way you look? Are you afraid of being ignored?

3. Get comfortable with the uncomfortable

One way to get outside of your comfort zone is to expand it. Make it a goal to avoid running away from discomfort.

Let's stay on the theme of meeting people in social settings. If you start feeling a little panicky when talking to someone you've just met, try to stay with them for a little longer than you normally would before retreating to comfort. If you stay long enough and practice often enough, it will start to become less uncomfortable.

4. See failure as a teacher

Many of us are so afraid of failure that we would rather do nothing than take a shot at our dreams. Begin to treat failure as a teacher. What did you learn from the experience? How can you apply that lesson to your next adventure to increase your chance of success?

Help your mind understand that failure is not fatal. One of the best ways to accomplish this is to expose your mind to new possibilities. You do this by reading, listening, and watching people in similar situations talk about their journey to success.

As you listen to people talk about their successes and failures, you will start to realise two things:

First, the path to success is not as straight as you would have thought. People rarely share their difficulties, which can create a false feeling of failure because your life is not as perfect as theirs. The second thing you will realise is that failure is a part of success. You will be hard-pressed to find someone who has experienced success without experiencing opposition.

5. Take baby steps

Don't try to jump outside your comfort zone, you will likely become overwhelmed and jump right back in. Take small steps toward the fear you are trying to overcome. If you want to become better at something, you must start hanging out with the people who are doing what you want to do and start emulating them.

6. Believe you can

If you want to step out of your comfort zone, you must believe change is inevitable. If you don't believe you are going to succeed, chances are you won't. You must believe that you can learn and develop the skills necessary to better your life. Dealing with resistance to change starts in the mind. If you want to change your life for the better, you must believe it is possible and in your best interest to do so. It will seem scary at first to get out of your comfort zone. But as I said, you don't need to jump right out of your comfort zone at once, you can take baby steps gradually.

7. Don't forget to have fun

Learn to laugh at yourself when you make mistakes. Risk-taking will inevitably involve failure and setbacks that will sometimes make you look foolish to others. Be happy to roll with the punches when others poke fun.

Enjoy the process of stepping outside your safe boundaries. Enjoy the fun of discovering things about yourself that you may not have been aware of previously. As you slowly push past your comfort zone, you'll feel more and more at ease about the new stuff.

Take the first step and I'm sure you'll make it!

In any given moment we have two options: to step forward into growth or to step back into safety.

Abraham Maslow

Unleashing the Fire From Within

Fear gets to most of us, whether it is fear of failure, fear of success or even fear of fear. All of us have experienced fear at some point in our lives and it can be a real stumbling block that holds us back from being truly successful.

I have changed jobs more than twenty times in my career. More than once when I handed in my resignation and was serving my notice period, doubt crept in. I questioned myself: is the next job a good fit for me? Is the grass greener on the other side? Did I make the right decision? I feared the uncertainties that the new job brought.

Fear can't hold you back forever if you don't let it. There are several ways to overcome fear, here are my top eight:

1. Separate reality from perception

Ask yourself what is really going on, locate the facts and prioritise them over your feelings. I noticed that my fear during the job transition comes from the unknowns: new colleagues I have not yet met; the new company culture that I've never experienced; and the processes and systems that I am yet to navigate.

2. Identify the trigger

Figure out what it is in a situation that triggers you. Learning to identify it will help you combat it. For me, it's about the uncertainty the new job brings. But I won't be able to figure out the 'unknowns' until I land the new job. So, it's more likely a fear of fear.

3. Feel thankful for tiny things

Every day, list out 1-3 things you are thankful for. It doesn't matter how big or small it is, being grateful helps shift the mind into a positive light, which over time, overcomes fear.

After I shut down my laptop at the end of a work day, I get changed into my lounge clothes. I look back on what happened during the day and start to feel grateful for tiny things like the aroma of fresh ground coffee, and the subtle sound of flipping paper.

4. Don't say anything negative to yourself

Monitor your inner conversations, don't talk yourself down and don't say anything negative to yourself. If you wouldn't say it to a friend, don't say it to yourself. Speak positively to yourself and remind yourself of your strengths.

When I find my mind drifting to negativity, I go outside, stand tall, close my eyes, breath in and out deeply, and then open my eyes.

Try to observe your environment and find one thing that you didn't notice yesterday. Your time is better spent living in the present than going down the rabbit hole of negative thoughts.

5. Practice breathing exercises

Breathing helps centre our body. My favourite breathing exercise is a simple breathwork of five deep, long breaths at any point to calm and centre myself. It is best to start the day with this, but when I start to get stressed, I practice this any time during the day.

Focus on the length of your inhalations, holds, and exhalations, really help you get out of your head and stay present. This breathwork style is often referred to as 4-7-8 breathing, and it goes just like that.

In a calm and quiet environment, find a comfortable seat or place to lie down or sit straight. You can keep your hands on your lap, lying down by your sides, or consider placing one hand on your belly and one on your heart.

And now start counting…

- **4 – Begin to inhale, quickly and deeply over four seconds.**

- **7 – Once four seconds of inhalation have passed hold your breath for seven seconds.**

- **8 – Then release your exhalation, slowly and precisely over eight seconds.**

And Repeat!

6. Mini yoga break

Yoga is a powerful tool to fight fear, stress and anxiety, visualise my day and be more productive. Although I don't always have time for a full yoga session, I'll insert a mini yoga break into my day. Whenever I feel fear of something, I'll find a quiet spot (inside or outside), stand still and pay attention to different parts of my body and try tiny movements with different body parts, notice the weight in my feet, wriggle my fingers, relax my shoulder, stand up taller, lengthen my neck. These tiny movements help me find peace of mind and make me feel refreshed and energised.

I learned that courage was not the absence of fear, but the triumph over it.

Nelson Mandela

Scan the QR code or visit thedreamlifeproject.co website for additional resources, including downloadable journals, meditations and podcasts.

Design

Life is a precious gift, and to make the most of it, it is essential to take ownership and actively shape our path. Goal designing plays a crucial role in this process, allowing us to define our aspirations, set a clear direction, and take meaningful actions towards the life we desire. By setting meaningful goals, we seize control of our destiny and embark on a journey of personal growth. It is a transformative practice that empowers us to take ownership of our lives. By setting clear goals, we stay focused and actively shape our destiny. We unlock our potential, cultivate resilience, and create a life of purpose. Seize the opportunity to design your goals, take control of your life, and embark on a journey of self-discovery and personal excellence.

Why Goal-Setting Is the Secret to Success

"Why should we set goals? Life is happening to us anyway, and what matters is if we can be happy now."

That was the beginning of an interesting conversation I had recently. And I totally agree that we must learn how to be happy here and now. Be happy with who we are, what we have and what we are doing.

We all have these basic needs to fulfil so that we move forward in life. This, in turn, means we have a choice: to choose which of two types of people we are. The type who sets their goals for moving forward consciously or the other type who does that unconsciously.

The majority of people fall into the second category. They set their goals unconsciously and reactively depending on what happens in their life. This is not wrong but is most probably an obstacle for them to be successful and feel happy.

In that line of thought, I have a friend who likes to say that our destiny is already written and no matter what we plan and do, "what's going to happen will happen." I like to say that the lessons we need to learn in life are probably written down but the path to learning them depends on us.

Happiness is found along the way, not at the end of the road.

Setting goals is not only about the result but about the experiences and lessons we learn along the way. We will have to change our plans many times and goals may not turn out exactly as we initially wished them to.

Setting goals is important, it sets an intention on which path we want to take. When we achieve our goals, we gain confidence to further make bigger progress and become a better version of ourselves. However, it should not be a reason to wait for the result to feel happy. Many people postpone their happiness for a future moment even when they have achieved their goals.

Unfortunately, that approach never works. "If only I had, if only I could, when I have time, when I have money, when I find the right partner, when I have kids, when my kids grow up." Those are traps we all fall into sooner or later.

Happiness is not a goal, it is a by-product.

I remember when I was a kid and wanted a new bike so badly. "I will be so happy if only I could have this bike." Then, my parents bought it as a present for me and I was really happy to have the bike. Of course, that was temporary.

Happiness doesn't only come with the result, it is in our everyday life, and it depends on our inner perception of ourselves and our own defined success. It is important to keep achieving our goals so we can gain confidence, motivation and energy to continue forward and make great things in life.

Happiness can be achieved through training the mind.

I would like to share with you my five strategies on how goal designing helps me to live a happier life.

1. Measure your success against what you've already achieved

We all have dreams, wishes or big lifetime goals we would like to achieve. That will be great if you have clarity on what they are and use them to motivate and direct yourself in life.

The tricky part is to measure yourself against the small steps you've already made on the road of your journey. This way, you will see your achievements, feel successful, gain confidence and feel positive in all perspectives of life.

If you measure yourself against the ideal future you wish to have, you will get to the opposite. You will constantly see a huge distance and thus feel unsuccessful and unhappy even though you may have achieved great things in life.

2. Become aware of your thoughts and be present

You cannot stop thinking, but you can train yourself to be more aware of your thoughts and stay present. When you find yourself wandering in thought, don't judge yourself, but be grateful for being aware and "awakening" again.

Pay attention to what your thoughts were about. If you don't like it or you find it a waste of time, you can just let those thoughts go away and start to shift your focus back on what you are doing at the moment.

3. Do what you say or change your agreement

Be aware of your commitments. Sometimes we make commitments and don't even realise we are doing so. Or we make commitments just because we don't feel comfortable saying NO. In both cases, you need to remember or write down what you promised.

Second, if you see that you won't be able to do what you said, or it will not be on time, negotiate and change your agreement. Go and tell the person you won't be able to finish what you promised. If that person is you, then change the agreement with yourself.

4. Choose larger life goals and dream bigger

The happiest people on the planet are those who have goals larger than themselves and live with a positive attitude toward making something valuable and good for the world.

Choosing larger goals and dreaming bigger is a process you can start right now. Get as clear as possible about your dreams. They are important because your dreams are what will help you get through tough times and give you the motivation to keep moving forward.

5. Track your progress and celebrate success

Write down your goals and be clear on which of them can fit into the 10-year vision category and the 90-day action goal category. Then start checking your progress daily and continually celebrate your progress.

Once you have achieved your goals, acknowledge that and celebrate your success. Journal all achievements, big or small, and whatever excites you. Your day might not always go as planned, but that does not mean there weren't little or big wins to celebrate.

You can't go back and change the beginning, but you can start where you are and change the ending.

CS Lewis

Taking Ownership of Your Life

Have you ever thought to yourself that there aren't enough hours in the day or felt overwhelmed by the tasks you have to face?

If you have, you are not alone.

We all get the same 24 hours, so why do some people seem to achieve more with their time than others? The answer: good time management.

Time management is the process of organising and planning how to divide your time between different activities. Get it right, and you'll end up working smarter, not harder, to get more done in less time, even when time is tight and pressures are high.

When you know how to manage your time effectively, you can unlock many benefits. These include:

- **Greater productivity and efficiency**

- **Less stress**

- **A better professional reputation**

- **Increased chances of advancement**

- **More opportunities to achieve your life and career goals**

Overall, you start feeling more in control, with the confidence to choose how best to use your time. Good time management shifts your focus from activities to results. Being busy isn't the same as being efficient and effective.

So, how can you best manage your time to make the most of it?

1. Planning is key

Planning is a simple but relentlessly powerful mantra of time management. It starts with creating a list of your tasks and then distributing them in the most appropriate way across your week. You can even preview the order in which you aim to go through the pending work in your day, as well as the breaks you want to take in-between tasks.

2. Reduce distractions in your workflow

Efficient time management depends on reducing distractions. Eliminating distractions, like checking social media, is far too ambitious, but restricting the time you dedicate to them is possible. You can turn distractions into a treat after each accomplishment in your day.

3. Learn to delegate

One of the main causes of exhaustion and burnout is the inability to let go of tasks, meaning saying 'yes' to too many things. Delegation is priceless when it comes to your personal time management.

The first steps can be difficult if you're not used to surrendering responsibility. However, you should find the balance between your healthy diligence and the unhealthy feeling that you're the only person who can get the job done. With time, this will improve your relationships with partners, colleagues or teammates, and delegating tasks will come naturally.

4. Embrace doing one task at a time

And defend it relentlessly. One of the biggest sources of stress today is multitasking. While a few years back multi-tasking was seen as a top skill, nowadays people have come to realise this approach has detrimental effects on productivity, concentration, and overall wellbeing.

It's useful to close your mailbox and social media channel and work on the task at hand only. You can also restrict calls and other potential distractions. Then you can set time slots for focusing.

5. Plan breaks between work streams

Having breaks between different activities is essential for keeping your brain fresh and escaping mental overload. When you're planning time slots for different tasks, it makes sense to also schedule breaks for stretching and snacks.

For example, if you have to work on legal contracts all morning, it's good to plan a short break before you dive into writing emails. This will give you a chance to do the mental jump and will help you prevent exhaustion. However, it's best if it is not related to using any of your digital devices, so that you can have some screen-free downtime.

6. Find your work pace

Over time, you should discover the right work tempo that fits your personality. You can achieve this by paying attention to the hours when you're the most productive, as well as to the moments when your energy and concentration go down. In a journal, log your most productive hours and least productive hours to check efficiency throughout the day. By analysing the data and being aware of how you feel, you can discover what needs to be altered in your daily routine to maximise productivity and reduce stress.

7. Set agendas for work meetings

For many of us, a big chunk of our daily work time goes into meetings. Whether you're a freelancer, a small business owner, or a team leader, you're probably facing the same situation. Because meetings are time-consuming (but important), you need to make sure that you are well-prepared for each one.

First, make sure that each meeting you agree to is truly necessary. Sometimes a call or a chat can serve the same purpose. Once you establish that the meeting is important, then you should prepare a clear agenda of what you expect to accomplish from it.

8. Learn to refuse work

Saying 'no' is a healthy mechanism that we need in most areas of life. When it comes to work, however, it can be the approach that saves you from burnout. If you're swamped with work and you can see that extra tasks will lead you to burnout, your best bet is to be straightforward about where your limits are. You should learn to say 'no'.

9. Analyse your daily habits

Take a step further in managing your time by analysing your habits. It's useful to take a close look at the rest of your activities beyond work.

If you're working from home and not from an office, you can take a look at how often you find distractions in household tasks or jump to the fridge for snack breaks. In the case of office work, you can pay attention to your rituals, and any unnecessary interactions with colleagues. Once you have a good overview, you can figure out how you can eliminate excessive distractions.

10. Incorporate exercise into your day

Exercise helps you better cope with stress and feel more relaxed. The first step is to find time for it in your schedule. The best approach is to have training sessions before your working hours. You can add stretching or yoga breaks throughout the day as well. If you're just getting started, begin with easy exercises, like walking, that you feel comfortable with, and expand gradually.

11. Diversify your routine

If you feel stuck in your everyday routine, take a step back and figure out what can bring some freshness to it. You can work from home if you've been in the office for too long. Try rearranging your working space as well. You can also start the day with exercise or reorder the typical way of planning your working hours.

Effective time management means less stress. When you know that you can manage your time to get things done, the buzz in your head is reduced, leaving space for concentration and relaxation. Instead of scattering your hours on side tasks, with good time management, you can redirect this time and dedicate it to the essential stuff that you want to complete. This is how you can align your goals with real-life efforts.

You have brains in your head. You have feet in your shoes. You can steer yourself any direction you choose. You're on your own. And you know what you know. And you are the one who'll decide where to go.

Dr. Seuss, Oh, The Places You'll Go!

Planning Your Time Mindfully

If you ask me how I manage my time, how I organise my time so that I get the important things done well, how I balance my time between different activities, and how I focus on the important things? My answer is mindful planning.

When I notice I'm going off the track, I ask myself the following questions:

- **Do I often interrupt working on a task to answer emails, calls or chats?**

- **Do I often feel like I don't know where my day went?**

- **Do I get negative feedback on my projects?**

- **Do I often miss deadlines?**

- **Do I feel overwhelmed by the number of pending tasks I have?**

- **Do I feel like I'm losing control over my workflow, or even my life?**

If you have more than one yes, then there's a big chance that you're not planning your time in the best way possible. The benefits of mindful time planning include greater productivity, less stress, and more opportunities to do the things that matter.

Ultimately, good time management will translate into a better ability to make important decisions. Why? Simply because you'll have more headspace. When you have clarity over your work and a solid plan on how to achieve each goal, you free up your potential for imagination, creative thinking and problem-solving.

When it comes to mindful time management, I have a few tips to help you get started.

1. Prioritisation is key

The way you create your action plan should be based on a thorough understanding of your goals and their priority. Once you have identified the different levels of importance and urgency, you should stack the essential ones at the top of your to-do list. By doing this, you can prevent losing track of their status or postponing them unnecessarily.

2. Conduct time management audits

If you want to know where your time goes throughout the day, your best helper is the time management audit. It's very easy to prepare and its benefits are many. There are various time audit templates online to start with.

Write down how you plan to use your time during a certain week or month. Then, track the hours each day and note what kind of activities you complete. When you have real-life data, you can easily compare whether your intentions match what you accomplish in your working time. After that, you can make the necessary adjustments to your priorities so that you gradually bring together your targets and your actual daily schedule.

3. Work on similar tasks together

This tip is tightly linked with the previous one. Instead of scattering different tasks across the day, it's more effective to group tasks of the same kind together. By doing this, you can save time by completing them at once.

4. Do the most important tasks first thing in the morning

Mornings are the most productive time of the day. Even if you don't feel fully awake yet, your brain is fresh and able to process information in a much better way. It's best to use this time for the most complex tasks or the ones that need the highest level of focus.

5. Know when to stop

You may be tempted to continue working on a task because it's in flow, especially if you feel they are important or complicated. However, you should learn to set limits and when to stop.

Seeking perfection is admirable and a powerful quality, but it can become an enemy to your mindful time management. As you tackle more projects, you'll get better at the time needed to complete different tasks, and when you're just wasting time trying to make it more 'perfect', then you should put a stop to that task.

6. Don't work on holidays and weekends

That's a strict rule that you should respect. The only work-related thing that is worth tackling on a weekend is planning. It may take you a bit of time, but it'll pay off during the week.

Working while on a holiday or weekend will build up stress, and this potentially leads to burnout. The best thing to do is leave work at work.

7. Use time management apps

Several apps can help you streamline your workflow. A calendar is a good starting point for your planning, as you can visually arrange your tasks for the week and month. You can input projects and tasks, add information, and set deadlines for completion. Having a time-tracking app will help you with your time audits and overall planning.

8. Change your landscape now and then

Changing scenery is a preferred method for rekindling creativity for writers and artists, but it also works for all types of professionals.

When you get the first signs of anxiety, boredom or mental overload, hit the road. If you don't have days off, or if a project can't be abandoned right now, then just change the landscape. It can be your cottage, a day in the park, or a trip to the beach; any place that will give you a breath of fresh air.

Your time is limited, so don't waste it living someone else's life.

Steve Jobs

Unstuck Yourself

How often do you feel like you are not at 100%? Sometimes I feel less than great. I feel my energy level is low, I'm grouchy, fed-up and bored. Days like those are part of life. We are not always living our dream life. There will always be off days, and that's okay.

But what happens when you get a whole string of those off days, sometimes it might be a few weeks, months or even years? Many of us say that we're in a rut and admit that we don't want things to be that way, but we don't know how to change.

I used to feel like I was in a rut and had no clue how to get out of it. Then I started to try building new healthy habits, and they improved my life significantly. I wake up every day, knowing that I am truly living my true purpose in life.

Here are some fun and easy ways you can use to climb, or better yet, leap out of the rut and start to live a dream life.

1. Build a new habit

Start with making one or two simple changes to your day, be it your podcast list, gym workout, route to work, lunch menu, etc. Don't worry about what the changes are or whether they're right or wrong, just make a couple of simple changes that will serve you well.

Doing something differently or changing parts of your routine instantly takes you out of the norm and allows you to shake off the things that make you feel confined. Step out of your routine and you'll be in a position to make different choices, diversify your perspective and get an alternative result.

2. Start with small steps

It can seem daunting to start small, but if you break that sizeable long-term goal down into smaller steps and start on just one of them, then the task seems easier. If you challenge yourself to achieve a modest goal at first, you can grow from there, once you're ready. Reaching a small, more achievable personal development goal empowers and encourages you to continue. It gives you confidence and empowers you to achieve bigger dreams.

3. Go at your own pace

As well as starting small, you shouldn't pressure yourself to achieve something in an unrealistically short timeframe. We often overcommit, so if you can't reach your goal in the time you have allowed, be kind to yourself and relax the deadline.

4. Focus on your strengths

Too often you focus on your negatives. You concentrate on learning something new, but sometimes you might want to consider improving something you're already good at, rather than addressing one of your weaknesses. Honing in on your current skills and applying them in a new area is easier than learning a new skill altogether.

5. Have a winner's mindset

It's never wrong to embrace and address your failures. But if you go into new experiences and learning situations with a winning mindset, you are more likely to do so. Believe your abilities can be developed over time through experience and learning. Don't worry about how smart you are, how you look, or what a mistake might mean. The key is to believe you are a winner, the challenges you encounter are just headwinds in your journey, and you will reach your destination one day.

6. Learn from others

If you pay close attention, most people you come across day to day can teach you something that you can then apply in your own life. You might come across a friendly barista when you pick up your morning coffee who's attention to detail will probably brighten your day. Can you then apply that attitude in your next encounter and make someone else similarly happy? Try to also be open to new opinions and new ways of doing things; you never know what you might learn.

7. Celebrate every little win

Celebrating your achievement along the way keeps you motivated. Write down all of your achievements, big or small, and whatever excites you. Yesterday has come to a close, and the next day is yet to be unveiled. It might not always go as planned, but that does not mean there weren't little or big wins to celebrate.

Don't forget your reward. It can be as big as an overseas holiday when you win a million-dollar project, or as small as a chocolate brownie for your consecutive three-day gym workout.

Every day you have the power to choose a better history — by opening your hearts and minds — by speaking up for what you know is right.

Michelle Obama

Scan the QR code or visit thedreamlifeproject.co website for additional resources, including downloadable journals, meditations and podcasts.

Declutter

In the chaos of modern life, our minds and physical surroundings often become cluttered with the burdens of accumulated thoughts, possessions, and distractions. Decluttering our mental and physical space offers a profound opportunity to find joy in life. By freeing ourselves from the burdens of excess thoughts, emotional baggage and unnecessary possessions, we create room for serenity, clarity and authentic happiness. Decluttering can liberate us from the weight of excess and invite happiness into our lives. Embrace the liberation decluttering brings and rediscover the joy that resides within yourself, and your surroundings.

Decluttering Your Physical and Mental Space

We need to protect our peace regardless of the chaos we face every day. Every one of us has mental, emotional and physical clutter that hinders us from seeing the good things in life. This is why it is important that we organise our space, both physical and mental, and revaluate the way we see, feel and respond to things and other events in our lives.

Have you ever experienced feeling so relaxed and focused because of how tidy your physical environment is? This is the best analogy I can ever give to those people who are still not convinced that decluttering will greatly impact their life. It helps you unblock the positive energy and instead attracts more space for abundance, happiness, and the realisation of your dreams.

Clutter makes a mess in your head. It's the cumulative effect of being around clutter that can drain your brain and make it harder for you to focus. The long-term effects of these things include depression, fatigue and high levels of the stress hormone, cortisol. With conditions like these standing in your way, your mental health begins to deteriorate, making you much less likely to deal with the clutter head-on.

Physical Clutter

Physical clutter is whatever messy and unnecessary things you see in your surroundings. Having an unorganised working area or environment deteriorates your energy and affects your mood.

I know everyone can relate to this: when I was still a child, it was very annoying to hear my mother scream at me to clean my closet or my room. For me, it was such a chore and a waste of time as my room would return to its cluttered state after a few days. Now, after learning that these physical clutters, such as unarranged clothes or disorganised files, in my surroundings can affect my mood and my focus, I have learned to appreciate the lesson which my mother was trying to inculcate in me.

Studies show that physical clutter you see every day, be it your closet or messy desk, takes up most of your focus and attention. Thus, instead of focusing on your work or attracting positive energy, this clutter competes for your attention, which often results in you not giving your full mind to whatever task you are doing.

Mental and Emotional Clutter

Mental and emotional clutter is an uneasy feeling that prevents you from functioning to your fullest. It can be doubt, fear and regret that prevents you from moving forward and keeping a high head while facing life.

You should keep this mental and emotional clutter in check because cleaning your physical environment is only half of the story. You should learn to declutter physically, mentally and emotionally. Regardless of how tidy your physical environment is, if your inner self is disturbed and restless, everything will still stay in a shaky place.

Organise Your Surroundings

Seeing clutter everywhere requires excessive stimuli which exhaust your mind. Clutter indicates to your brain that there is still something to be done. Thus, your mind cannot get the relaxation that it needs to focus on other important things.

Looking for something in the clutter can be frustrating, especially if you don't know where to start. So, make sure that you have a place for everything so that you can find them easily. This will not only save you time but also lessen the pressure and stress on your mind.

Let Go of the Unnecessary

Most of us have something that we cannot just let go, maybe because of its sentimental value. We do not want to let go of the memory or the hope for the future, be it an old pair of shoes that we cannot find the perfect occasion for or a certain memory still lingering within us.

Only keep what you currently need. Stop holding onto things you do not need. There is no point in dwelling on a past feeling or memory if it only brings you uneasy feelings in the present time. You have to remember that there are already so many physical, mental and emotional battles you are fighting every day. There is no need to add another battle that does not matter.

Know When Enough is Enough

With the technological advancement that we are enjoying nowadays, we tend to multitask a lot and overload ourselves. However, multitasking only reduces the efficiency of your brain to produce quality work. Plus, it only adds to the pressure and stress that you have to overcome.

Learn the art of doing single tasks and saying no so you will be able to focus more. Avoid doing too many things at a time because it does not guarantee quality. You may be able to complete your projects sooner, but you will still not feel satisfied because your focus is divided, and your attention distracted.

Retreat with Nature

We don't often notice the small things as we are so focused on running after our deadlines. So, take a walk. Notice how the flowers bloom and hear the chirping of the birds during sunrise. Take everything easy and experience life in slow motion.

One of the best ways to declutter your mind and your soul is to be with nature, away from the city traffic and away from technology. This is to ensure that you will have your much needed "me time" without any distractions.

Regain Self-Love

In addition to spending time with nature, it is also best that you indulge yourself with whatever it is that makes you happy. Spend your lazy Saturday afternoons in a spa or treat yourself to that chocolate cake.

Showing how you love yourself will improve how you see things and your relationship with the inner you. Also, this will make you feel grounded in your desires and goals in life. It will help you redirect your focus to the things that truly matter.

Tidying is the act of confronting yourself; cleaning is the act of confronting nature.

Marie Kondo

Say Goodbye to Procrastination

You put off your exercise routine until tomorrow. You continually delay finishing that project or starting that business. Procrastination is the mother of all demons and can stop you from achieving all that you desire.

I've been putting off writing this book for almost a year! There was always something that popped up whenever I started writing; a sudden increase in workload, laptop malfunctions, or a fire alarm in my building, and so on. After one year of battling, I designed a plan to help me commit and find time for writing.

Here, I share four effective processes. You can use them to stay on track, no matter what things you are putting off.

1. Set your intention

Hold your breath and jump right in! Putting things off until the last minute is a bad habit. Like all other habits, this is ingrained in your subconscious mind and hard to break. Take a moment to set mindful intentions and clarify your needs before a hectic day is unveiled. Take a chance to pay full attention to your true needs, desires, wants, and the 'why'.

Focus on your purpose. The most important thing is to be clear on your goals and what you want to achieve. It helps you set an intention for the day, find your why, get out of the bed and drive on. Even though you have to put things off and give priority to what is urgent, you can get back on track quickly.

2. Take one step at a time

Sometimes, we procrastinate because the task is intimidating. In these cases, we need to take one step at a time. You need to break down the project into smaller pieces and tackle each bit separately. Make each task an individual project, and after completion of each one, celebrate and acknowledge your achievement.

When you're trying to build a new habit, it's easy to start too big. Even when you know you should start small, it's still easy to start too big. When all we hear about are other people's spectacular results, it's natural to think that we need to push ourselves to the limit to achieve anything worthwhile. I know, I've made that mistake many times myself.

If I have to recommend one tactic to start when building a new habit, I would say choose a habit that is as easy as possible to perform.

The most effective way to do this is to follow the "Two-Minute Rule." When you start a new habit, it should take less than two minutes to do.

For example:

"Walk 10,000 steps each day" becomes "Put on my running shoes."

"Keep the house tidy" becomes "put one item of dirty clothing in the laundry."

"Get straight A's" becomes "set my books out on the desk when I get home."

The idea is to make your habits as easy as possible to start. The Two-Minute Rule helps counterbalance our tendency to bite off more than we can chew. Make it easy to start and the rest will follow.

Even broad life goals can be transformed into a two-minute behaviour. Wanting to live a healthy life may be your ultimate ambition, but then you can ask "what do I need to live a healthy life?" I need to stay in shape. Then you can ask "what do I need to stay in shape?" I need to exercise. "What do I need to do to exercise?" I need to change into my workout clothes. And so on until you get to a behaviour that takes two minutes or less.

3. Make it convenient

Think about something that you have been putting off again and again and again. What are the reasons that you need to complete this task in the first place? What are your reasons for this lengthy delay? I find it amazing that 99% of the time I put off doing something because I found it too hard to stick with it.

The less friction associated with a habit, the more likely it is to occur. In other words, as convenience increases, so do the odds that you follow through on your habit.

When deciding where to practice a new habit, it is best to choose a place that is already along the path of your daily routine. Habits are easier to build when they fit into the flow of your life. For example, you are more likely to go to the gym if it is on your way to work because stopping doesn't add much friction to your lifestyle.

Perhaps even more effective is reducing the friction within your home or office. For example, put together a home gym setup. That way, even if you don't have time to get a full workout at the gym, you can still do a few sets at home.

4. Build a tribe

Do you put off tasks because you feel that they are too big and complex for you to handle alone? Get a tribe together, you don't have to do it all by yourself. If you're surrounded by readers, you're more likely to consider reading to be a common habit. If you're surrounded by people who recycle, you're more likely to start recycling too.

My friends who exercise daily tell me that it is much easier to do with someone else. When you're working out alone, you can give up whenever your mind wanders. When you're working out with a friend and 10 minutes pass, you don't want to be the first one to quit. You'll keep going for the entire time.

If we wait until we're ready, we'll be waiting for the rest of our lives.

Lemony Snicket

Good Habits Will Propel Your Dream Life

Your dream life is made up of a series of good habits. A good habit is a behaviour that is beneficial to your physical or mental health, often linked to a high level of discipline and self-control.

You may be surprised to learn that more than 40% of the actions you perform every day aren't decided by you. They're habits. Habits dictate how we live, how we perform, and the results we achieve in life. This is why it is essential to have strong, positive habits.

The most important part of building a new habit is staying consistent. It doesn't matter how well you perform on any individual day. Sustained effort is what makes the real difference.

To live my dream life, I have four types of habits: wellness, kindness, mindfulness and sustainability.

Wellness

Wellness is self-love and self-care as a whole. It is making choices that lead you to feel your best! To enjoy and accept the wild ride of life, wellness empowers you to make the best possible choices for your mind and body health. Wellness is the act of practising healthy habits to attain better physical and mental health outcomes so that instead of just surviving, you are thriving.

Wellness provides you with a safe and compassionate way to bring self-love back into your lifestyle. It serves as a tool to help you maintain a positive mental and emotional attitude through physical exercise. By building wellness habits, you can yield numerous benefits as they contribute to your strength, endurance and intelligence, both physically and mentally. It always works as a continuous support system, even in passing moments of discomfort, life challenges, and adverse situations.

Some ideas for wellness habits:

- **A daily yoga class in a studio or at home.**

- **A one-minute plank a day. Start with as long as you can hold, then add more each time.**

- **Walk 10,000 steps a day.**

- **Run for 1 minute then walk for 1 minute – continue this for 10 minutes daily.**

- **Drink a glass of lemon water every morning.**

Kindness

Kindness can mean different things to different people. The meaning is in how you choose to show it. Be it through empathy, acceptance, kind gestures, and thoughtfulness, the possibilities are entirely up to you. Kindness might look like being helpful, showing empathy or doing nice things without expecting anything in return.

Kindness takes practice to understand and feel it. We share our love with others through kind acts; a smile, a nice word, an unexpected deed, or a planned surprise. When you offer these acts to others, you make people feel good, pass along hope, promote peace and show the power of kindness. It's in your nature to learn by watching others, which is why it is so important to be kind to yourself and show kindness to those around you.

Some ideas for kindness habits:

- **Write a card to someone every single day.**

- **Give at least one person a compliment every day.**

- **Send a photo a day to your parents/grandparents/ loved ones.**

- **Write down three things you're grateful for.**

- **Smile in the mirror once a day.**

Mindfulness

Mindfulness means living in the present moment by maintaining a moment-by-moment awareness of your thoughts, feelings, bodily sensations and surrounding environment. It connects you with your inner sacred heart through daily mindful habits. Mindfulness also involves acceptance, meaning that you pay attention to your thoughts and feelings without judging them. By practising active mindfulness throughout the day, you slowly develop habits so you feel more ease during the frustrations and challenges that everyday life can bring.

Being mindful will help you become compassionate and find contentment. When you practice mindfulness, your thoughts tune into what you're sensing in the present moment rather than rehashing the past or imagining the future. You learn to connect yourselves with the practice of being present.

Some ideas for mindfulness habits:

- **Say an inspiring mantra/affirmation daily.**

- **Eat lunch and dinner slowly every day with no phone or TV.**

- **10 minutes of daily meditation.**

- **Pause work and take 10 deep breaths a few times every day.**

- **Set an intention for the day before you go to work each morning.**

Sustainability

Sustainability is the habit that nurtures all living beings. It is more than just buying eco; it is a commitment to a sustainable lifestyle. By including sustainable and eco-friendly habits into your lifestyle, you actively work on restoring compassion and loving-kindness, to be good for the planet, the environment and the people and places around you.

A sustainable lifestyle means you intentionally use natural and clean resources, foresee the future, predict the path you are heading on now, and mindfully prepare for a thriving and healthy life. You build habits centred on long-term sustainability, through everyday responsible actions and the continuous intention to support life.

Some ideas for sustainability habits:

- **Buy groceries from a local produce market and cook at home.**

- **Organise one drawer/cupboard/shelf in your home each day.**

- **Remove one item from your life each day to minimise clutter; recycle, donate or resell it.**

- **Save $10 a day.**

- **Try plant-based milk in your coffee.**

If you don't know where to start building a new habit, ask yourself these six questions. Below each question is my answer to inspire you.

What is the one habit that I want to track?

- **I want to write one page/one chapter of my book every day.**

When will I be doing my daily habit?

- **I will write at least one thousand words in my book after my morning coffee every day.**

Why am I doing it?

- **Because I want to complete the manuscript and get my book published in one year.**

What obstacles are likely to come up?

- **My 9 to 5 job sometimes requires me to join an early morning meeting, so I won't be able to stick to this routine every day.**

How will I overcome these obstacles?

- **As soon as I finished with the early morning meeting and my No.1 priorities for that day, I'll take time to write.**

My reward?

- **My reward is the excitement of holding my hardcover book in my hands.**

Today is your day.
To start fresh.
To eat right.
To train hard.
To live healthy.
To be proud.

Bonnie Pfiester

Building and Maintaining Good Habits

Now that you have a few ideas of good habits, the next question will be 'How to build and maintain good habits?'

Habits are repetitive pattens of your lifestyle. Maintaining habits is the brain's way of being more efficient. As far as the brain is concerned, the more tasks you can complete without wasting time thinking about them, the better.

I tested these eight steps to maintain healthy habits, and they work. Follow them when you have a go.

1. Eliminate triggers

Identify the people, places and activities that are linked in your mind to bad habits. Then change your behaviour toward those.

For instance, if you have a shopping addiction, avoid going to the shopping centre. If you want to quit smoking, don't go outside when your friends take a smoke break.

Chronic stress can also trigger poor behaviour. Make sure to actively manage your stress levels to avoid triggers.

2. Reduce cravings

Cravings stem from a desire to change your internal state. This means you can reduce cravings by identifying how you want to feel. Then, use a healthier action to achieve that feeling.

For instance, if you're craving relaxation, take a bath instead of smoking. If you're craving energy, eat a banana instead of drinking your third cup of coffee for the day.

3. Make a negative habit difficult

Habits can only exist if the behaviour is easy enough to engage in. If you make the behaviour difficult, you won't be able to do it. For instance, if you have a bad habit of staying up too late, start work earlier in the morning.

If you know you'll be physically exhausted and running on a few hours of sleep, you'll think twice before staying up late.

4. Uncover the root

Uncovering the root of your bad habits is one of the most important ways to change them. For instance, maybe you'll discover that you stress eat because you need coping tools.

Knowing that a lack of coping tools is the root of your habit, you can nurture your mental wellbeing in better ways. For instance, you can use self-care practices like mindful breathing to cope with stress.

5. Adopt healthy routines

Building good habits boils down to lifestyle choices, and one of the best ways to change your lifestyle is by improving your daily routine. Map out your day and integrate healthy practices where they make sense.

6. Create a supportive environment

Surround yourself with like-minded people who have similar goals to you. As humans, we are greatly influenced by what others around us are doing or feeling.

Being around a positive group of people who share similar goals and interests to you can be the single greatest catalyst to help you maintain your habit.

Tell your family, friends and colleagues that you plan to maintain your new habit. Sharing your habit goals provides accountability and support for your habit maintenance.

7. Check in with yourself to be sure you're on the right track

As you move toward developing healthier habits, pay special attention to how you feel as you incorporate them into your life. Does your new practice seem to fit with your lifestyle and personality? Is it easy to maintain your new habit, or do you think you may need to try something new?

If you find that you haven't kept up with your new plans as you've hoped, rather than beating yourself up over it, congratulate yourself for noticing that you need to change or modify your plans. If you're trudging along, but have decided that you really need to try something else instead, at least you know what doesn't work for you. Now you can try something else that you may end up loving.

Great things are done by a series of small things brought together.

Vincent Van Gogh

Unearthing Your Passions in Life

Not every moment of your life is exciting and full of meaning. You won't do every task with a big smile on your face. Life isn't sunshine and roses all the time. All paths have good and bad moments, and pursuing your passions won't always be easy.

You'll sometimes feel confused and frustrated in your journey toward finding what you love. You won't be able to devote as much time to it as you'd like. If you love what you do, you will look forward to starting your day, even if it's not always with a smile.

Doing what you love is even good for your physical and mental health. When you engage in doing things that you love, you experience less stress and have a lower resting heart rate. It helps instil calmness throughout your body. Not to mention it injects more positive thoughts into your mind and helps to banish negative ones.

In the case of finding a dream job and great work opportunities, it doesn't come without any effort. When I was changing jobs, 1 encountered three key work orientations. A job, career path, and passion will provide me with different experiences while finding what I love to do.

None of them is necessarily right or wrong; there aren't any perfect answers on this journey. Maybe your job doesn't fulfil you entirely, but it still provides some joy. Or, your career path could be full of hard work to earn promotions, but it doesn't fulfil you.

This journey isn't linear, just like many other things in life. It's full of ups and downs, but your resilient mindset and hard work will still teach you things along the way and help you find passion.

To develop a passion, you have to engage with it. The more you get to know it, the more you'll uncover interesting problems, quirks, and challenges that pique your interest and love.

Here are eight steps to help you learn what you love to do:

1. Read new books or articles about people who have found their passions

Perhaps their passions aren't the same as yours, but you'll pick up new strategies and tips along the way. Reading other people's stories is also a source of inspiration for you to continue on your own journey.

2. Get career advice from entrepreneurs and professionals

Listening to career advice might point you in a direction you never thought of before. Soaking up expert advice will also help build your confidence and empower you to make moves with your career path.

3. Listen to podcasts about motivation

Some days you need a little extra motivation to put a spring in your step. While you're doing activities like exercising, commuting or even cleaning, put on a podcast that makes you feel energised to take action.

4. Follow social media accounts that post about following your dreams

If you spend a fair amount of time scrolling through social media posts, why not scroll through those that empower you to follow your dreams? The more you read posts about finding your purpose or meaning in life, the more you'll be focused on working toward achieving it.

5. Save money where you can so that you can focus on your passions

Finding what you love to do might have a price tag attached to it, so saving money will help with that. It'll also teach you how to budget your finances and be more intentional with your pay checks.

6. Write down a list of your strengths and refer to it often

Writing down and reviewing your strengths will remind you of what you're great at. Knowing your strengths will help uplift you after a bad day and reassure you that you're capable of achieving your goals.

7. Think about what you wanted to be as a child

You might have flip-flopped between a few different future career aspirations as a child. But go back and think hard about why you thought of those possible careers in the first place. It'll give you insight into your interests and remind you of your first loves.

8. Make a list of your dislikes

Just as it's valuable to know what you like, the same goes for your dislikes. It helps you cross off possible passions and narrow down your list. Knowing what you don't like also saves your energy for pursuing your passions and finding what you love.

Fall in love with taking care of yourself; mind, body, and soul. There is only one of you. You are truly once in a lifetime.

Latisha Cotto

Loving What You Do

It feels good to love what you do. Your passion is the reason you get out of bed every morning, and you look forward so much to starting your day.

I have been searching for a dream job for the past 20 years. There is no doubt that a dream job will get you driving on the darkest and hardest days. It makes all the difference. You don't dread your tasks or daydream about escaping. The work you're doing has you completely engaged and immersed. Maybe it's what you've dreamed of achieving or maybe it's a surprise to you that you find it so compelling.

Either way, you're excited to start. Your energy becomes magnetic when you love what you do. You attract like-minded individuals who share your passion for hard work and achieve an excellent work-life balance.

Reasons to do what you love

You deserve to do things in life that you love, period. Think about it the other way: why should you only do things that don't make you feel passionate, interested or fulfilled? A meaningful life oozes passion and love.

If you need any more reasons to pursue what you love, here are five to review:

- You'll be more fulfilled in your personal and professional life because you're pursuing your passions.

- You'll be more productive with your work.

- You'll serve as a positive role model because people will feel inspired by your hard work and values.

- You'll be more open to learning new things because you'll want to expand your knowledge and skills.

- You'll spend less time procrastinating because when you do what you enjoy, work of any kind doesn't feel like a chore.

You make choices every day. Some of those choices lead you to love what you do, while others don't. Here are six habits you can use to work towards loving your work and enriching your life:

1. Pay attention to the details

It's nice to have big ideas and visions of how you want your life to look, but when you love what you do, the more minor details are more meaningful.

Focusing on the details requires putting extra effort into what you're doing. Entrepreneurs know that rather than being careless, they need to be intentional and think each element of their work through. It's done with love, even though it might mean spending more time on each task.

2. Bring in all of your energy

Have you ever looked at someone and wondered where they get all of their energy from? Here's a hint: it involves passion and love for their work. When you're working on a project that excites you, your energy is a giveaway. Working your dream job will elevate your energy and encourage others to do the same. Next time you start a project that makes you excited to get to work, don't let anyone tell you to take it easy. Allow yourself and your energy for what it is rather than being bashful about it.

3. Try new things

Trying new things is how we discover what we love. Before trying them, you didn't know your favourite foods, so apply this approach to new jobs. Change is good, even if it scares you a bit. If you have a particular job or industry you want to work in, try connecting with people in that industry for career advice. Cruise around LinkedIn for a co-founder of a business you admire or any other successful person and ask if they have any tips. If they're passionate about what they do, rest assured, they will love to talk about it.

4. Appreciate your mistakes

Making mistakes can be frustrating, annoying, and disheartening. But when you view them as learning opportunities, they can do much more good than bad for your wellbeing. Your mistakes are pockets of information and great learning opportunities. They can tell you what strategies don't work and give you clues as to what might be best for you.

5. Strategize wisely

You want your actions to be meaningful. To do great work, you need a solid plan. Think about all the factors you need to align to accomplish your goals. Sit down and write them out step by step. If you want to build a personal brand online, ask yourself which social media platforms will work best for you. Then, research any tools that help with social media posting so you can plan your strategy thoughtfully.

6. Keep your habits and goals sustainable

While on the road to loving what you do, you need to be honest with yourself. If your to-do list is unattainable, you won't feel productive or admire what you're accomplishing. Habits and goals fit into people's lives in different ways.

Some personal goals are more attainable in the given time frame than others. Think about what realistic goals you can start implementing without stressing yourself out. Doing what you like needs to be sustainable or else it'll be short-lived, and that's not what you're setting out to achieve. Sustainable goals are easier to meet, and meeting your goals motivates you to achieve more.

7. Make your work environment enjoyable

A work environment you feel motivated in will help make your life meaningful. Waking up to go to work in the morning will be exciting, and you'll feel rewarded after doing some good work. Think about the impact your efforts will have on others. Make friends at work so you have someone you like to chat with over lunch. Whatever makes you feel excited to sit at your computer (in the office or at home) matters.

8. Be in the present

When you do what you like and like what you do, you want to experience it fully. Make sure to enjoy your time. Relish in your accomplishments and be proud of yourself. The more you appreciate what you're doing, the more you'll love it. You do this by staying in the present. Of course, you can still set long-term goals and think about the future, but don't forget to savour what you're currently experiencing.

There comes a time when you ought to start doing what you want. Take a job that you love. You will jump out of bed in the morning. I think you are out of your mind if you keep taking jobs that you don't like because you think it will look good on your resume.

Warren Buffet

The Dream Life Project

Scan the QR code or visit thedreamlifeproject.co website for additional resources, including downloadable journals, meditations and podcasts.

Devise

In the hustle and bustle of modern life, it's easy to get caught up in a cycle of busyness and distraction, missing out on the richness and depth that life has to offer. However, by cultivating mindful habits, we can unlock the fullness of life and experience each moment with greater presence, joy, and gratitude. Mindful habits hold the key to unlocking the fullness of life. They can lead to a profound transformation and a deeper appreciation of the world around us. By incorporating practices that promote presence, gratitude and intentional living, we learn to savour the richness of each moment, connect deeply with ourselves and others, and embrace the full spectrum of life's joys and challenges.

Unlocking the Fullness of Life with Gratitude

"Gratitude unlocks the fullness of life. It turns what we have into enough, and more. It turns denial into acceptance, chaos to order, and confusion into clarity. It can turn a meal into a feast, a house into a home, a stranger into a friend." This is my favourite quote from Melody Beattie.

Our days are busy. It's easy to spend each one rushing from one thing to the next, filling the in-between moments with mindless scrolling or mental to-do lists. When life is hectic, we tend to focus on what we lack: what we don't have, what isn't working, and so on. Plus, the tough stuff of life can so easily spiral from a bad day to a hard week to overall feeling low and disappointed in where life has us.

However, if we choose to see it, our days are also overflowing with goodness, splitting little seams of blessings. You can ignore these moments, or you can collect them, savour them and say thank you!! Though we don't get to choose our circumstances, we do get to choose our outlook.

The practice of gratitude is a major stress buster. It reduces a multitude of toxic emotions, from resentment and envy to regret and frustration.

It also keeps us present. When I practise gratitude, I look around me and feel so thankful for clean water in my water bottle, and a beautiful and inspiring space to work in. When I'm sitting there thinking about all the things thankful for, I don't get overwhelmed with jealousy at someone else's success. Anytime I'm feeling less than others, or I start to be bitten by the comparison bug, I try to step back and think of three to five things I'm grateful for. It works for jobs, relationships, finances, material comparison and more!

How To Inject Gratitude Into Your Every Day

1. Try a one-minute gratitude break

Instead of constantly scrolling on my phone when I'm waiting in line, I like to intentionally set my phone aside, take a deep breath and start listing in my mind the things that I'm grateful for or what are bringing me joy that day.

It's usually just a few minutes of productivity "sacrificed" for something that is actually more valuable and connective. Even that little bit of time reaps major benefits in your overall sensation and frame of mind. It's a great trick to use when you're feeling especially anxious or stressed.

2. Start a gratitude journal

I recently started writing down three things I feel thankful for every day. It has created such a positive practice in my life, especially in hard times. Every morning or evening, write down a few things that you're thankful for. There's no right or wrong answer, it can be anything from your family to the person that let you go ahead in line at the grocery store. Over time, the habit of giving a name to all the good things in your life reduces stress and produces a more positive outlook.

Here are some journal prompts to help you get started:

- **What are three great things that happened yesterday?**
- **What are 30 things that bring you joy?**
- **What are you looking forward to right now? If you can't think of anything, what can you do to change that?**
- **What is one totally free thing that's transformed your life?**
- **What things in your life would you describe as "priceless"?**
- **What are 10 things you're actively enjoying about life right now?**
- **Write about the most fun you had recently. What were you doing and who were you with?**
- **Write about an act of kindness that someone did for you that took you by surprise.**

- **What are some of your favourite ways to show the people in your life that you love them?**

3. Say "thank you" to someone

Think of one person who's made a positive difference in your life. Whether a mentor, colleague, friend or inspiring boss, we all have people in our lives who have shaped us for the better. When we express our thanks, we introduce positivity into our environment and spread those good vibes to other people. Silent gratitude doesn't mean very much to anyone. Telling a person outright what they mean to you goes a long way, blessing you and the other person!

If you are a little shy, a handwritten thank you note says a million words. Nothing warms someone's heart better than reading the handwriting and telling them how important they are in your life. When words are written down from pen to paper, both the recipient and you can feel the warmth. You both will understand how gratitude helps you see things differently, in a positive way.

4. Gratitude rituals

Create simple rituals that allow you to express gratitude regularly. This could be saying a gratitude prayer before meals, having a gratitude jar where you add notes of appreciation, or setting aside a specific time each day to verbally share what you are grateful for with a loved one. Rituals help make gratitude a consistent part of your life.

Set up a gratitude jar where you can jot down notes of appreciation on small pieces of paper. Each day or week, write down something you are grateful for and place it in the jar. Over time, the jar becomes a visual reminder of the abundance in your life and can be revisited whenever you need a boost of gratitude.

5. Gratitude meditation

Practice gratitude through meditation. Find a calm and quiet space, focus on your breath, and bring to mind things you are grateful for. It can be a person, a situation, a quality, or anything that brings a sense of appreciation. As you bring that person or thing to mind, allow yourself to deeply feel the gratitude and appreciation it brings you. Notice any sensations, emotions or thoughts associated with it.

Optimists find joy in small things. They are more concerned with having many small joys rather than having one huge joy.

Robert M. Sherfield

Living in the Moment

How can we start living in the moment in a world that is constantly trying to draw our attention to the past and future? Before we get into concrete actions we can take, it's important to understand what mindfulness is. You've probably heard the term before but may not fully understand what it means.

To be mindful is to live in the moment.

When you are mindful, your attention is focused on what is happening in the present moment, and you are fully in touch with reality. You are aware of what is happening in your body, mind, emotions and the world around you.

With mindfulness, you calm your mind and emotions so you can see clearer. To develop mindfulness, you need to train yourself to observe things more objectively, that is, without your emotions or preconceived ideas influencing your views.

When you adjust your relationship with time and find your centre, you can take ownership of your commitments and your life. Here's some simple techniques you can use to live in the moment:

1. Take time out

If you're hustling 24/7, it wreaks havoc on your mental and physical wellbeing. It's crucial to carve out some downtime to slow down and breathe. Bring a book to read in the park or take a long walk without your phone.

2. Discover what you want

Make a list of all the things you want to do, including exercise, personal time, family time, stretching, yoga, etc. Take a look and make sure it reflects your desire for self-care. If you did these things, would you feel calmer and happier? If so, add them to your calendar and prioritise them.

3. Allow space to digest thoughts and emotions

When you aren't digesting your thoughts, you create a backlog of mental suffering that keeps you from being present with your friends and family. To fix this, allow time to process your feelings. A hike in nature is a great time to work through that emotional turbulence, in turn allowing you to be more present for the rest of your life.

4. Sweat it out

Sitting is the new smoking, it harms your health as badly as smoking does. Get up and move around frequently throughout the day to improve your body's functions and overall sense of wellbeing.

5. Eating meals as a ritual

Our ancestors spent hours preparing meals and enjoying them with loved ones. We should return to seeing mealtime as an opportunity to slow down and nourish our bodies, absorb nutrients and relax into the digestive process.

6. Communication isn't what it used to be

Today, a vast amount of our communication is electronic. But it's important to interact face-to-face to establish a personal connection. Set up more in-person communications, focusing on things like body language and eye contact. See how much better you feel.

7. Rearrange your workspace

Work can swallow your time and prevent you from properly caring for yourselves. If you rearrange your workspace a bit, you'll give yourself more room to think outside the box. Spatial awareness cues your bodies to stay more awake and wires your brain to work more efficiently.

8. Daydreams give you new insights

Block off some time to think about a trip you'd like to take, and imagine the sights, sounds and textures. Building positive and productive daydreaming into your life can be therapeutic and inspiring

9. Turn off notifications

We created technology to help us save time and energy, but constant alerts, reminders and notifications take us out of the present. Take a hard look at your relationship with technology and see where you can cut back.

10. Don't let social media become a tick

Check social media only once or twice a day after you've completed your important tasks or have a social media blackout day to reset your mind.

11. Take five deep breaths

Set a timer for every two hours. Whenever it pings, stop what you're doing and take five deep breaths. Focus on slowing the inhale and holding for a second at the top of the breath. Then release a long, deep exhale. When you train your body and mind to press pause and nourish your breath regularly, you feel calmer.

12. Soak up some sun

We all need sunlight to trigger vitamin D synthesis and balance our neurotransmitters. Make a concerted effort to spend time in the sun to reap the benefits.

13. Get up and stretch

Take a five-minute break once every two hours. Get up and stretch, or do some yoga, whatever gets your blood flowing. Listen to your body and let it decompress. Practising this throughout the day will keep your oxygen pumping to give you more energy.

14. Books can take you out of time and space

Books give you information, insight and knowledge, and take you to new places. Today, pick up a book you've been meaning to read and get through at least 30 pages. Relax into the experience and know it's time well spent.

15. Enjoy a moment with a neighbour

Back in the day, we used to be close to the people who lived in close proximity. Today, it's just a quick smile or wave as we pass in the driveway. Making an effort to connect with the people around you will make you feel less lonely and improve your mood.

Enjoy the little things, for one day you may look back and realise they were the big things.

Robert Brault

Let Yourself Flow

We often hear people talk about the importance of living in the moment and the different ways it will benefit us. It all sounds wonderful, especially since it can help with lowering levels of stress and anxiety, but how exactly can we live in the present when our minds are constantly worrying about the past or planning for the future?

First things first, why do we worry?

Before we answer this question, it's important to distinguish between worry and concern.

When we are concerned about something, we are more likely dealing with a real problem with realistic solutions. Then, once we do whatever we can to address the problem, we're willing to live with the outcome.

Worry, on the other hand, involves unrealistic thinking. We may worry about a problem that doesn't exist or dwell on all the bad things that can happen as a result. Then, we feel unable to deal with the outcome. We find it difficult to deal with uncertainty, which is a normal part of life.

While it can be difficult to stop worrying and start living in the moment, it has innumerable benefits.

Better Health

By reducing stress and anxiety, you avoid many of the associated health consequences, such as high blood pressure, heart disease and obesity. Studies have shown that being present in the moment can also improve psychological wellbeing.

Improve Your Relationships

Have you ever been with someone who is physically present but mentally a million miles away?

Being with unavailable people is a struggle, and building relationships with them is extremely difficult. How about being with someone who is fully present? We enjoy being with them because we can make a much deeper connection.

By living in the moment, you can be that person other people enjoy being with, and you will make relationships much easier.

Greater Self-Control

You have greater control over your mind, body and emotions when you are living in the moment. Imagine how much better your life would be if it weren't at the mercy of a racing mind and unpredictable emotions. You would certainly be more at peace and much happier.

Why Should You Stop Worrying Too Much?

There is often way too much talk of building for the future, but what about building for the now? We all desire genuine happiness, and in order to manifest this joy, we have to live presently.

Too much focus on the future often leads to stress and negative thinking.

Here are five reasons why you should stop worrying and feel more in the flow:

1. The present moment is the only moment you have control of

No matter how much you worry, you never know how life is going to play out. The only time you will know is when you are in that moment.

The moment you are experiencing right now is the only moment you can control. You can choose to enjoy the moment, or you can choose to loathe the moment. You can also choose to ignore the moment completely and waste it away, but either way, the present moment is yours to control.

Worry isn't going to take you out of the present. It is not going to improve your quality of life. It isn't going to guarantee you a desired future outcome. So, why not accept what you can control now?

2. Each moment is a gift

There is no guarantee on the number of moments you will get to experience. Your next moment is not predictable, so why not take advantage of the one you are in?

You can't live with this unique perspective if you are constantly worrying about the next stage of your life. You can only experience this zest for life if you are living in the present moment. It may even sound corny and unrealistic, but it makes perfect sense.

Don't take moments for granted. Plan when it is necessary but not at the expense of enjoying the present moment. As the old cliche saying goes, life is short, so enjoy it while you can.

3. Being present is a great stress reducer

Thinking too much about the future, and the past, is often the cause of stress. Even though some stress can be beneficial, the stress caused by not living in the moment can be detrimental to your mental, physical and emotional health.

Invigorate your life with present living strategies that will enable you to stay more focused on each moment. You probably don't have the luxury of meditating one hour a day and not setting some type of plan for your future, but implementing small changes to your life should help reduce stress.

Observe when your mind begins to focus on the future instead of the present moment you are experiencing. Ask yourself if this thought process is necessary. Simple awareness and recognition of your thoughts will assist you in being more present.

4. Plans often don't manifest themselves the way you want or expect

How many times have you tried planning something but it just didn't work out the way you wanted? How did you react? Did you get upset or did you handle the situation with acceptance and understanding?

Plans fail sometimes. It is a part of life.

Attempting to plan for every step of your life is impossible. The more you plan, the more likely you are to become irritated or upset when those plans don't come to fruition.

I am not suggesting you shouldn't plan with the attitude that the plan will fail, but I am proposing that you let life run its course and just be. Go ahead and make plans if that is helpful for you, but don't lose sight of the present moment. If your plans don't work out the way you want, then at least try to accept them.

5. Living in the present will make you happier

Living in the present is one of the sure-fire methods you can adopt to manifest genuine happiness in your life. Don't impede yourself from experiencing contentment. Practice living in the present and observe how it makes you feel. The moment you have right now is a gift. Enjoy less stress by relishing the moment. Accept the present for what it is and be happy.

Plan as you feel necessary. Save money for a family and house. Invest in yourself. Set goals for yourself and realise them. That is what you are supposed to do, but in this pursuit don't forget about where you are in the present.

For every minute you are angry you lose sixty seconds of happiness.

Ralph Waldo Emerson

Meditating for 10 Minutes Every Day

Meditation can help you learn to notice your thoughts and actions instead of just getting lost in the narrative and, as a result, become less reactive and more compassionate toward yourself and others.

When we sit to meditate, we are looking after ourselves in ways that might not at first seem obvious. Two years ago, I started meditation to manage stress, reduce anxiety and cultivate peace of mind. But there are thousands of studies documenting other less-known meditation benefits, which can have a positive impact on mental, physical and emotional health.

Meditation is the habitual process of training your mind to focus and redirect your thoughts.

You can use it to increase awareness of yourself and your surroundings. Many people think of it as a way to reduce stress and develop concentration. You can also use the practice to develop other beneficial habits and feelings, such as a positive mood and outlook, self-discipline, healthy sleep patterns and even increased pain tolerance.

The most significant benefits of meditation include:

1. Lower stress

Perhaps the most common reason why people practice meditation is to lower their level of stress. Ample studies have shown that regular practice of meditation can relieve stress and improve quality of life.

Stress, whether caused by mental or physical reasons, if not managed, can be harmful. These can lead to high blood pressure, anxiety, insomnia, depression, loss of concentration and fatigue. Research shows that meditation can benefit stress relief and improvement of other stress-related disorders.

2. Reduces anxiety

Meditation allows you to cope and react positively to anxiety, whether or not it is brought on by specific stressors. In order to attain anxiety-relieving benefits, you should practice meditation regularly.

3. Enhances mental health

Some types of meditation can lead to improved self-confidence and a positive outlook on life. Studies show that regular meditation can lower the symptoms of depression, reduce the frequency of negative thoughts and generate more positivity in life.

4. Improve self-awareness

Meditation is one of the best ways to improve self-awareness. Regular meditation helps you develop a better understanding of yourself. It reduces the feeling of loneliness and brings contentment.

5. Increases concentration and attention span

Regular meditation is known to increase focus and the duration of your attention span. People who practice meditation tend to be more focused and accurate when completing a task. Enhanced attention and memory can be derived even after practising meditation for just 10 minutes a day.

6. Generates empathy and kindness

People who practice meditation tend to have more empathy and kindness towards others. They tend to impart positive feelings to others, are quick to forgive, and move on with life. Overall, meditation tends to improve interpersonal interactions and exudes positivity.

7. Improves sleeping

Another benefit of regular meditation is that it improves sleeping. If you struggle with sleep, then meditation can help you achieve deep sleep faster and stay asleep longer. Plus, meditation is known to relax the body, ease tension in the muscles and induce a peaceful state, all factors that are necessary for good quality sleep.

8. Lower pain

The perception of pain is closely linked to the mind and can be elevated when you are under stress. Research shows that meditation can help increase the pain threshold and/or reduce the perception of pain in the brain. In the long run, this also leads to an improved quality of life and a better mood.

9. Lower blood pressure

Meditation is known to lower blood pressure by easing stress and reducing strain on the heart. Countless studies have shown that regular meditation can slightly lower blood pressure or reduce the need for blood pressure medications, hence reduce the risk of a heart attack and stroke.

Although meditation is powerful, for some people, it's difficult to get into the zone and shut off their thoughts. Here's how to get there:

1. Don't give up

Meditation is a powerful tool to fight stress and anxiety, visualise your day and be more productive. Find a quiet spot, either inside or out, stand still and pay attention to different parts of your body and try tiny movements with your body. Notice the weight in your feet, wriggle your fingers, relax your shoulders, stand up taller and lengthen your neck. These tiny movements will help you find peace of mind, refreshing and energising.

2. Meditate throughout the day

Accept that your mind can be distracted during a long meditation. Instead, you may do shorter sessions throughout the day. It can help you forget about your worries, be more focused at work and regain a sense of calm. Three or four moments of distraction-free thought can help you banish stress and anxiety, and improve your overall health.

3. Try guided meditations

If you find your mind drifting somewhere every other minute, guided meditations can help you bring back your focus. Over the years, I've tried several guided meditation programs and apps, and I found the following work the best:

- **Buddhify**

Buddhify promises peace of mind for the cost of a cup of coffee. It's a convenient meditation app with a beautiful design that will help you reduce stress, be present and get better sleep.

- **Calm**

Calm will teach you meditation techniques for sleep and stress relief. There's also a great soundtrack of white noise, water, and other calming and soothing sounds.

- **Headspace**

Headspace is scientifically proven to reduce stress and anxiety. You can adapt the program to your busy lifestyle and make time to do the activities, which will help you focus and relax.

- **Mindful in May**

Mindful in May will transform your mind and life. It provides education, tools and support so you can build a sustainable meditation practice to become mentally fit in one month.

- **Danielle LaPorte**

Danielle LaPorte's meditations are highly visual journeys designed to heal your nervous systems, open your hearts, and be a means of serving the collective and Mother Earth—which in turn opens your own channels to Higher Consciousness and Love.

- **Melissa Ambrosini**

Melissa's meditation will inspire you to unlock your full potential, reclaim your power, live with intention and move in the direction of your dreams. Transformation is possible for everyone.

You will never change your life until you change something you do daily. The secret of your success is found in your daily routine.

John C Maxwell

Working Out for 30 Minutes in the Morning

A morning workout is a top joy for me. It instantly helps me wake up, improves blood circulation, and keeps me warm during chilly winter days. Over the years, it has helped me build a strong mind. Life throws at us many things that are out of our control. But there is only one we can certainly take control of, and that is our own wellness. Plus, shredding a few kilos of body fat.

The human body was designed to move, and when it's deprived of this movement, the results can manifest as poor physical health, mood disorders and accelerated aging. Regular exercise is a highly effective way to relieve stress, anxiety and depression. Staying inactive accelerates the loss of muscle tissue, leading to weakness, increased risks of injury and reduced coordination. It also ages our brain by contributing to memory loss and brain fog.

We spend most of our lives sitting down at work or on the couch or lying down sleeping. Let's bring a little movement back, morning by morning, until it becomes a habit; as it should be.

How 30 Minutes a Day Can Change Your Life

Exercise boosts circulation, muscle strength, and endorphin production, helping your body work more efficiently. Simple tasks such as walking up the stairs and washing your car will feel easier. You'll also be more focused at work, less fatigued, less reliant on caffeine and more capable of accomplishing tasks throughout each day.

Gradually, regular exercise increases your muscle mass and helps you shed excess fat and fluids. As moderate daily exercise supports your body's production of antibodies and white blood cells, it will also fight off viruses and other pathogens more efficiently, significantly boosting your immune response and ability to fight disease.

I'm sharing my tips to help you get the most out of your workout and motivate you to keep going:

1. Make a plan

Create a personalised exercise plan and outline the steps you need to take to reach your health and fitness goals. Begin by devising a four-week schedule of workouts you want to do and stick to it. When it's time for each workout, you won't have to waste time figuring out what to do for that day—just refer to your plan.

2. Cross-train

Switch up your workout occasionally to strengthen different muscle groups, making you stronger and more powerful. No matter what your fitness level is, you'll always benefit from variety. Incorporate aerobic exercise, strength training, core exercises, stretching and balance. This can be as simple as taking a new yoga class or climbing lessons or topping your aerobic workout with 5 to 10 minutes of stretching, sit-ups and push-ups.

3. Forget your excuses

Since the beginning of the global pandemic, all of us spent a lot of time at home. There is no reason why you can't do workouts at home. Home is the warmest and cosiest place with your own surroundings. Every morning, I tune into a workout video by Emi Wong on YouTube. She has never failed to lift my body and my mind.

4. Start by being mindful of how you move

Take note of your movements. Moving your body is one of the greatest things you can do to improve your health. Let's start with some easy movements and notice how you feel:

- **Child pose** – knees folded underneath you, head on the floor, and arms by your sides or stretched out in front of you for two minutes. It's a great way to stretch your back, relax your neck and practice carving out time devoted to your body.

- **Neck and shoulder movement** – begin by moving your head from left to right then up and down for five minutes. Roll your shoulders backwards and forwards. Tip your head forwards and rest your hands on the back of your neck to release tension.

- **Bridge pose to work your lower back** – lie on your back with your arms by your sides, knees bent and feet flat on the floor. Slowly raise your hips, contracting your glutes and hamstrings as you go. Keep your shoulders on the floor. Hold for 10-15 seconds, then repeat five times.

- **Legs up on the wall** – lie on the floor with your legs extended against a wall. This pose will encourage blood flow and lymphatic drainage towards your heart.

- **Calve stretch** – plant your toes on the edge of a step and slowly let your heels dip down. Stretch each for five minutes.

- **Plank** – now take your body and mind to the next level! This pose is great for your core and your focus. Hold a plank for one minute, rest for 30 seconds, and repeat 5 times. If you found that too easy, double the length of your plank each round.

5. Write down how you feel

Track your workout length and intensity every morning. Notice how you feel, whether it's harder or easier than yesterday, whether one side of your body stretches, and whether your mind is begging you to give up or craving for more challenging workouts. Open up your notebook and write down your high praise.

6. Drink coffee after your workout (not before)

Working out each morning can give you that extra boost you need to set you up for the rest of the day. Morning workouts have been shown to improve focus and ability throughout the rest of the day. Over a while, you will notice your caffeine intake decrease.

Exercise in the morning will improve your metabolism, meaning that after you have finished your workout, you are still burning calories even just being sat at your work desk or sitting in traffic. A win-win situation!

The greater the obstacle, the more glory in overcoming it.

Moliere

Scan the QR code or visit thedreamlifeproject.co website for additional resources, including downloadable journals, meditations and podcasts.

Develop

Creating a dream life is not just about personal achievements, it also involves nurturing meaningful connections and making a positive impact on the world around us. By developing a comprehensive plan to care for ourselves, and others, we lay the groundwork for a fulfilling and purpose-driven journey towards our dreams. By incorporating self-care practices, cultivating empathy, volunteering, creating a support network, and regularly evaluating and adjusting our plan, we create a blueprint that fosters personal fulfilment and positive contributions to the lives of others. Caring for ourselves and others is a transformative step towards building a dream life. Let us embark on this journey of caring for ourselves and others for a dream life that is rich in purpose, joy and meaningful connections.

Regaining Self-Love

Self-love is an important part of self-care. The concept of self-love is simple: it just means valuing and caring for your own needs, wants and desires. It isn't about being selfish. It's about making sure you have time to recharge to have the energy and resources to be there for others.

As airlines like to remind us, it's important to put on your own oxygen mask before helping others do the same. Because if you run out of air, it becomes a lot harder to help anyone, including yourself.

Loving yourself can be one of the hardest, yet most important things you'll ever do.

What does it mean to love yourself? And how do you actually love yourself?

For various reasons, many of us find it easier to love others than to love ourselves. Sometimes we're quite harsh to ourselves. We subject ourselves to a harsh inner critic, unhealthy relationships, toxic substances and self-mutilation. I know how easy it is to dwell on your own perceived inadequacies.

It's time to start caring for yourself and treating yourself with the same love that you give to others. Loving yourself isn't selfish, as many fear. Not only does it improve your relationship with yourself, but it shows others how to love you.

You are the one person that you'll always be with. So, it's important that you enjoy your own company. Your relationship with yourself is the most important and longest relationship you'll ever have. It's worth spending the time and effort to develop a more loving relationship with yourself.

Now, I will share my list of the different ways to love myself. Many are simple and straight-forward. Some are harder. You don't have to use all of these ideas, but you'll find many overlap and work nicely together.

1. **Know yourself. It's impossible to love yourself if you don't even know who you are. Invest in discovering what you believe, value and like.**

2. **Say "no" when you need to. Boundaries are an essential form of self-care because they let others know that you deserve and expect respect.**

3. **Don't compare yourself to others. Others aren't better or worse, more or less than you. They're just different. You have value just as you are, and accepting yourself means there's no need for comparisons.**

4. Be truly present. Our lives are full of distractions. Many of these things are fun and worthwhile, but they can be draining and keep us from truly knowing and being ourselves.

5. Know and use your strengths. We all have tremendous gifts, but many of them go unnoticed. When you're busy and distracted, it's hard to access these great qualities. Focusing on your strengths will increase your positive feelings for yourself.

6. Give yourself a treat. A treat is something special that you just give yourself. Unlike a reward, it doesn't have to be earned. Be good to yourself by giving yourself treats "just because."

7. Be honest with yourself. This one can be harder than it seems. Some of us are so good at self-deception that we don't even know we're doing it. Honesty is key in all relationships, and your relationship with yourself is no different.

8. Let yourself off the hook for your mistakes and imperfections. You're hard on yourself. You're probably harder on yourself than anybody

else. Cut yourself some slack and embrace your humanness. Mistakes are normal. Imperfections are part of what makes you, you.

9. Accept that some people won't like you. That's right, some people don't like you and that's OK. Don't waste your time trying to please people who are impossible to please or people who just aren't that important to you.

10. Write down your successes. I love this self-love activity because it creates a record of your accomplishments (big and small) that you can re-read whenever you're feeling low. Add to it and read your list on a daily basis for maximum benefit.

11. Take good care of your body. Good health is truly priceless. Give yourself the gift of feeling physically well; exercise regularly, eat healthily, drink water, get 7-8 hours of sleep, and limit alcohol and caffeine.

12. Pursue a hobby. Hobbies can be fun, relaxing, challenging, creative, athletic, social or educational.

Different hobbies meet different needs for us. Find something that meets your needs.

13. Stand up for yourself. Like boundaries, being assertive is a way of showing others that your opinions and needs matter. Loving yourself means you know your value and can communicate it to others.

14. Ask for help when you need it. Another part of taking care of yourself is recognising when you need help. Help isn't weak. It's human. We all need help at times.

15. Speak kindly to yourself. Talk to yourself like you'd talk to a loved one. Don't cut yourself down or criticise yourself.

16. Sometimes loving yourself means you have to end relationships with abusive or unkind people. Surround yourself with people who treat you with kindness and respect.

17. Allow yourself some downtime. It's time to slow down and allow your body and mind to rest. You

don't have to do it all. Prioritise what matters most and let go of any guilt you might have about saying no. Rest is rejuvenating and a basic form of self-care.

Which of these ideas will you try? I recommend starting with the activities that seem easiest to you. Practice one or two self-love activities for a week or two and then try one of the more challenging ones. You can build your repertoire of self-love activities over time.

And as you practice and build them into your routine, they will feel more natural and won't take as much thought or effort.

To love oneself is the beginning of a life-long romance.

Oscar Wilde

Eating For Your Health

When you're stressed out, the foods that you're turning to are most likely going to be traditional 'comfort' foods – think big meals, fatty foods, sweet foods and alcohol. Let's face it, we've all found some comfort in a tasty meal and a glass of wine when we've been stressed out or upset about something. However, this isn't a good solution.

When you're turning to unhealthy foods, you can feel better temporarily, but in the long run, you will feel worse. When your body isn't getting the right nutrition, you begin to feel less energetic, more lethargic, and in some cases less able to concentrate and focus. All of this can lead to even more stress.

Filling up on foods such as whole grains, leafy vegetables and lean proteins as the basic staples of your diet is the best way to ensure that your body gets the optimum amounts of nutrients to fight stress. When it comes to choosing the foods to eat, some have a range of great properties which help the body combat stress. Choosing these stress-busting foods will help to heal and calm your mind in the long-term, rather than providing a temporary fix.

- **Avocado** – Avocados contain higher levels of vitamin E, folate and beta-carotene than any other fruit, which boosts their stress-busting properties. However, be careful with portion control when eating avocado, as it is high in fat.

- **Blueberries** – Blueberries have some of the highest levels of antioxidants. They have been linked to a wide range of health benefits, including sharper cognition, better focus and a clearer mind – all of which can help you to better deal with stress.

- **Oatmeal** – Oatmeal is a great, filling comfort food. It also has a large number of healthy properties to make you feel better from the inside out. As a complex carbohydrate, eating oatmeal causes your brain to produce higher levels of the feel-good chemical, serotonin, helping you to feel calmer and less stressed.

- **Green Leafy Vegetables** – Along with helping to combat stress, leafy greens are full of nutrients and antioxidants which help to fight off disease and leave your body feeling healthier and more energised. Dark leafy greens, for example, spinach, are especially good for producing more mood-regulating neurotransmitters, such as serotonin, which is a 'feel-good' chemical.

- **Fermented Foods** – Fermented foods, such as yogurt, can help to keep your gut healthy, which in turn will help to improve your mental health and reduce stress levels. The beneficial bacteria found in fermented foods have a direct effect on your brain chemistry and transmit positive mood and behaviour-regulating signals to your brain via the vagus nerve.

- **Chamomile Tea** – What you're drinking can also alleviate or worsen the stress you're feeling. Chamomile tea has long been used as a natural bedtime soother. Test results from clinical trials showed that chamomile tea is effective in reducing the symptoms of generalised anxiety disorder.

When you rush through a meal, no matter what time of day it is or what kind of food you are eating, your digestive system can't keep up. When you eat fast, it can't trigger the signal to tell your brain that you're full. Inevitably, you overeat.

You will also be likely to suffer from serious heartburn or gastroesophageal reflux disease later on. Because when you eat too quickly, air gets into your stomach and overloads it. This is due to your stomach trying to catch up with the pace at which you were sending all that food down.

Eating slower and mindfully have many amazing benefits to your body. Taking at least 20 minutes to eat at a time, allows your digestive tract to get a head start in the process of digesting the food.

Eat mindfully and adapt the 20-minute eating habit.

1. Put down your utensils between bites

In between bites, set down your utensil. This small move forces you to slow down and really focus on checking in with your body to determine if you're full or not yet. It also allows sufficient time for your stomach to send the 'I'm already full' signals to your brain.

2. Try setting a minimum number of chews per bite

When you aren't breaking down your food into tiny pieces, it can be very challenging to digest later. Try to set a minimum number of chews per bite. This can be five or thirty-five, whatever feels best to you. Once you get into the habit, you won't even have to count anymore.

3. Find another slow eater and pace yourselves to them

If you found that your eating pace is different when you are eating with different people, you are probably trying to match up to the other people. Next time, be mindful that you don't have to mirror them to the point they are uncomfortable, just find some self-awareness and eat at your own pace.

4. Use smaller plates and bowls

It will automatically help you take care of portion size. Prepare smaller plates and cutlets to practice mindful eating. When you are developing the habit of turning inward and connecting with the present moment, using a portion of food might be a helpful way to do this.

5. Pay attention to how you feel before and after eating

Your mood can affect food intake, record you mood after you eat each meal and notice the patterns.

Savour the food on your plate for at least 20 minutes. Enjoy every bite you take and chew your food slowly and properly. Not only will it help with better digestion, but it will also keep you satiated for a longer period of time.

You'll find that you're more aware of the texture, flavour and smell of the food, making the meal more interesting and memorable. I hope these give you some ideas for your eating habits; 'you are what you eat' so make sure that first and foremost, you're filling yourself up with foods that are good for your health.

*Take care of your body.
It's the only place you
have to live.*

Jim Rohn

Preventing Burnout

At some point, we all feel overwhelmed at work. Regardless of your field or role, work can be stressful. However, if you are finding yourself persistently feeling overwhelmed, that can be a sign of burnout.

Burnout is a result of chronic and persistent feelings of stress. It can occur when we are constantly feeling overwhelmed and drained. Promptly addressing feeling overwhelmed at work is crucial to avoiding burnout down the road.

You can feel overwhelmed if you have various responsibilities and feel that you do not have the support, time, energy or means to accomplish what you feel they need to. Sometimes, you may also feel overwhelmed because you are going through a life transition or a traumatic event.

If you experience any of the following symptoms, you may have a burnout:

1. **Lack of motivation.**

2. **Lack of pleasure in the job.**

3. **Lack of belief in your ability to complete tasks (a sense of inefficacy).**

Now, I want to share my personal experience and tips to deal with burnout.

1. Pay attention to your feelings

Burnout is inseparable from emotion, and emotions are powerful clues to what is important to us. Paying attention to feelings that arise and when they come up can help you manage resentment, frustration and disillusionment before they turn into burnout.

2. Set boundaries

Set and maintain firm boundaries that mirror your current capacity for work. For those that struggle with people pleasing, this can be difficult. Remember that you know your limitations and needs best. Say NO to additional, non-urgent and unnecessary tasks when you are at capacity.

3. Sleep

Work on your sleep hygiene. You can start by creating a routine around sleep. Experts recommend 6-8 hours of sleep per night. Not just to rest your bodies, but to rejuvenate your minds. Sleeping is the time for your bodies to not just rest but heal.

4. Schedule breaks

Make sure to take breaks throughout the day, even if it's five minutes to stretch and walk around your office, listen to your favourite song, get some fresh air, and take a minute to just breathe. Creating mental distance from work, even if it's brief, gives us time to pause and reset.

5. Connect with your support network

It is easy for us to get lost in our own realities. Sometimes we might not even realise how overwhelmed we are. When you feel you have more people connected to you, you are able to manage stressful and traumatic events.

6. Keep work at work

Try to set and stick to a work schedule that allows you to handle other important priorities in your personal life in a way that feels balanced to you. You might even try physical boundaries, like locking your office, shutting down your laptop and getting changed into lounge clothes at the end of the day.

7. Cultivate interests outside of work

By definition, burnout is a work-related phenomenon, but our health in other areas of our lives contributes to our vibrancy at work. It's an important part of work-life balance. Having positive outlets can help you get through a stressful or frustrating time in your job.

8. It's okay to tell your manager that you're feeling burnt out

Many of us, especially women, grew up with a warning to never show weakness in our work life. Knowing when it's time to protect your mental health should be seen as a strength, but it can still feel stressful to share your workload needs with your manager.

I think it is totally okay to tell your manager that you are feeling overwhelmed! There are many people competing for your manager's attention, and they may be unaware of how you are feeling. Communicating your needs to your manager can provide an opportunity for you to re-prioritise tasks, manage deadlines and delegate tasks.

Keep in mind that you will also perform your best when you are feeling confident and stable; your mental health is an essential component of your performance at work.

Rest and self-care are so important. When you take time to replenish your spirit, it allows you to serve others from the overflow.

Eleanor Brownn

Uplifting Others to Create Positive Changes

We all want to live our dream life every day. However, that's not always the case. There are times in which we may feel stuck, we may be in a situation that we feel unhappy in, or we are lacking the motivation or extra push we need to create positive change in our life. Sometimes we are not even sure what it is that we want.

When I'm feeling low, I take a step back and try not to force it. That usually means that I'll leave where I am and do something to get it out of my head. Go for a walk, get a massage, and do a yoga and meditation session. I'll lean into self-care stuff which allows me to relax. The same should help most people when they feel low.

If you see a friend is feeling low, by cheering her up, you are also reminding yourself how life can go back on track. But what's the best way to cheer someone up? Showing love to your friend can be meaningful and helpful, and in doing so, you are also showing love to yourself. But if there's one thing you can count on, it is that you can bring a little light into their life.

Don't know where to start? Here are a few simple and caring tips to lift up others and create positive changes in someone's life.

1. Send a handwritten letter

Do this on looseleaf paper or beautiful stationery. The important thing is that it carries a personal message, it will put a smile on their face and shows that you're thinking of them. Keep the message simple; it can be an inspirational quote, a hand-drawn portrait or a happy memory you had together.

2. Offer to help with chores or errands

Doing a load of laundry, making a grocery store run, or just tidying up around the house can offer a lot of relief to someone who's depressed or grieving. They may not express it overtly, but they'll be very grateful for the help. By getting rid of some chores, you're helping them get one item ticked off their to-do list, which is usually the least favourite item.

3. Send them an uplifting song or playlist

Sometimes putting your thoughts into words is tough. Leave it to the pros by deferring to a favourite song, or better yet, a thoughtful playlist. It can be classic, cheerful, nostalgic—whatever your loved one needs to get them through a tough time. Music has the power to flip negativity into positivity.

4. Send them a feel-good podcast

Like music, podcasts are a great way to escape and pump good vibes into the brain. For someone in need, a feel-good podcast might be just what they need. Send them your favourite episodes to help them unwind and enjoy.

5. Send a bunch of beautiful flowers

A bouquet of flowers means a million words. The aroma can lift the mood instantly, and the freshly cut flowers deliver a sensation of nature. Who doesn't love flowers? Take it to the next level by adding a handwritten note.

6. Drop off a home-cooked meal

This is a classic move for a reason. Put your love for your friend into a hearty meal that'll nourish their body and soul. Make sure it's something hearty and easy to prepare so your friend doesn't have to exert any extra effort. It's all about the little things, and a ready-to-eat meal is surely something they'll appreciate.

7. ...Or a bag of sweets

Nothing ignites joy quite like a good dessert. In a time of need, sweet treats are both comforting and delicious. Dessert feeds the soul, and your friend will definitely appreciate the sentiment that comes with homemade goodies.

8. Pick up the phone

In this world of social media, it feels like we've forgotten how much more intimate it is to make a phone call. Hearing your voice and getting carried away in a 30-minute conversation can make all the difference to someone who's down in the dumps. Don't forget to listen to your friend and make sure they have an emotional outlet.

9. Surprise them with an outing

Though they might say they'd rather stay in, an impromptu movie, mounting hiking, park walking, a picnic, roller skating date or any outdoor activity might work better to lift their spirits. Show up at their door and don't take no for an answer! It's hard to say no to something out of routine, and it can be fun.

10. Give them animal cuddles

Pet therapy is a sweet thing. It's been proven that pet therapy can decrease stress levels, anxiety, fatigue, loneliness, and even physical pain. You just can't beat the love and joy received from a cuddly, furry friend. Go together to a cat or dog café, and cuddle the furry four-legged friends while enjoying a cuppa.

11. Have a staycation together

Show up with takeout, magazines, pyjamas and no intention of leaving anytime soon. They'll be so glad to have someone to kick back and relax with. A weekend getaway is priceless.

12. Get some fresh air

Take your friend on a walk, enjoy a meal with them outdoors, or simply open up some windows in their home to let in lots of fresh air. Even though it's a classic movie cliché, fresh air really does something that just helps brighten a dark day.

13. Bring them along to your next workout class

While it may be the last thing on their mind, bringing your friend along to a workout will make them feel good from the inside out. Not only does it show them that they're on your mind, but pumping up those endorphins is always a good way to boost your mood. Plus, the feeling of accomplishment after is one of life's greatest gifts.

We rise by lifting others.

Robert Ingersoll

Creating the Best Year of Your Life

Finally, we've come to the last chapter of The Dream Life Project. If you are reading this book in December, namely the end of the year, you are probably breathing a huge sigh of relief.

No matter which month you are living in, regardless of whether the past year was the best year of your life or you felt like you were living in the twilight zone, there's no better time than now to reflect on things you can do to make sure this year is the best year of your life.

There's no doubt that things will happen that are out of our control. None of us are immune to unexpected bouts of grief, sadness, etc. However, we can control how we think about life and our approach to day-to-day living.

While I'm writing the last chapters of this book, I've been doing a lot of reflection to figure out what I want this year to look like. I'm optimistic this will be an awesome year and I'm going to share some ways you can approach this year so you can have an awesome one too.

1. Learn from the past, but don't repeat it

Take some time to think about all of last year's experiences, and more importantly, hold on to all the lessons you learned from those experiences. Understand that everything that occurred last year was simply a result. Don't get caught up in labelling those results as good or bad.

Know that results are just feedback. Learn from any mistakes you made and commit not to repeat them. Learn from your successes but don't let yourself get too complacent or overconfident. The actions that made you successful last year may not be the same actions you need to take this year. Be open to new approaches.

2. Get rid of the old, and make room for the new

It's hard to plan for the future when things from the past are still pulling at you. If you're starting the new year with unfinished projects from last year, you need to clear those projects from your plate as soon as possible. By getting rid of the old, you make room for the new. Start by listing everything you have not finished, at work and home.

Once you have that list, go through it slowly and for each item, ask yourself whether you absolutely must finish it yourself; and if so, set a timeframe for getting it done; whether you can delegate it, or whether you should scrap it.

You should also clear your workspace and your home of any unnecessary clutter. Physical organisation has a tremendously positive effect on the mental organisation.

3. Put your goals in writing

Anything worth achieving is worth putting in writing. Make a list of the major goals that you'd like to achieve this year. Each of these goals should represent a significant milestone in the long-term vision for your life.

Once you have your goals in writing, put them in a place where you will see them every day. Give each goal a specific deadline and begin breaking down each of those goals into actionable steps you can take on a daily or weekly basis.

4. Exercise

We all know that regular exercise is fundamental to our overall wellbeing, and yet so few of us do it regularly. The unfortunate truth is that exercise is the one thing everyone knows they should be doing regularly, and it's often the first habit they drop when they get "too busy" with other things.

Exercise is not something you "have time for." It is something you make time for. It is also the one thing that provides you with strength, energy and vitality to be more effective in all the other areas of your life. Exercise is an investment in your health, your life, your longevity and your productivity. If you think of your daily grind as cutting down a tree, then exercise represents taking a moment to sharpen the saw.

5. Build new relationships

The people you know and work with have helped you get to where you are. To get to a new level, you will need to surround yourself with some new people. Make it a priority to cultivate new relationships with positive people both inside and outside of your community.

Offer to help others in any way that you can, and in exchange, you will find that others become more inclined to help you however they can. Successful people know the value of a good network. They spend years building and cultivating their network, and as a result, they are presented with fruitful opportunities and better positioned to take advantage of them as they come.

6. Learn new skills

New goals require new actions, and new actions typically require new skills. Take a moment to identify some of the skills you would like to acquire this year and begin looking for the people and resources that can help you acquire those skills.

Whether it's a local class, an online course or a seminar, remember that all skills are learnable. Don't make excuses for not learning new skills. People who stop learning new skills are the first ones to become obsolete in the marketplace.

7. Make balance a priority

If the next year is truly going to be your most successful year yet, then it must be successful in all areas of your life. You don't want this to be the year where you get a big promotion at work but your relationship with your spouse goes down the drain. You don't want this to be the year where your business thrives at the expense of your health.

Balance is about consistency. If you consistently invest in each area of your life—your career/business, your relationships, your health, your leisure, your spirituality, etc.—then these areas will thrive. If you consistently neglect any of these areas, they will suffer.

Just like with getting exercise, you don't "have time for it"—you make time for it. Remember that it's not about the amount of time you give to each area, it's about the quality of the time you give to each area. Some areas require several hours per day, and some will only require a few hours per week.

8. Hold yourself accountable

The last but perhaps most important point to ensure you make this year your best year is to hold yourself accountable. Lack of accountability is one of the single greatest reasons for failure. If no one is holding us accountable for the consistent implementation of new habits or behaviours, we are more likely to fall back into our old patterns.

The secret to holding yourself accountable is to have a system. Without a system for tracking your daily and weekly activities, and then measuring those against the new standards you've set for yourself, failure is almost inevitable. What gets measured, gets improved.

Give yourself permission to live a big life. Step into who you are meant to be. Stop playing small. You're meant for greater things.

Anon

Scan the QR code or visit thedreamlifeproject.co website for additional resources, including downloadable journals, meditations and podcasts.

One Last Thing

We all want to reach our dream life. We all want to live our best lives every day. We all want to grow, both personally and professionally, and fully experience what life has to offer, without the fear, stress, anxiety and everything negative.

As much as we want to thrive and succeed, sometimes we will fall off track. That's normal. This book will bring you back to the basics and remind you to stay on purpose.

The purpose of this book is to inspire you to build good habits so that you achieve your dream life. It provides many practical ideas and tips that you can apply in your everyday life. Always come back and check in for your daily dose of inspiration.

The second purpose of this book is to remind you that you are the one in the driver's seat, that you can live each day with intention, clarity and purpose, so it's up to you to truly engage and enjoy every aspect of your life.

I'm applauding your courage and celebrating your potential, as you take your first step towards your dream life.

Best,

Cecilia Huang

About the Author

After changing jobs 20 times in 17 years, Cecilia Huang learned that unleashing her 'why' and finding her purpose has helped her achieve her goals. Cecilia has done this by building good habits and staying positive, resilient and happy. Through her own experience, she empowers others to adapt towards and stay on track to living their dream lives.

Cecilia believes that every human deserves a simple, meaningful, happy, and purposeful life. She is passionate about helping people like you to stay true on purpose, whatever that is for you.

In The Dream Life Project, Cecilia share ideas and inspiration for living your dream life every day. Sharing personal takes, tips, and techniques to discover the 'why' in your life and build good habits to achieve it, Cecilia compels you to take your past experiences - the 'failures', the 'regrets', the 'weird times'- and thank yourself and move into a life you have dreamed of.

www.ingramcontent.com/pod-product-compliance
Lightning Source LLC
Chambersburg PA
CBHW041306110526
44590CB00028B/4258